Deception Detection

Deception Detection

*An Educator's
Guide to the
Art of Insight*

JEFFREY SCHRANK

Beacon Press Boston

This book is dedicated
with love
to my parents

Copyright © 1975 by Jeffrey Schrank
Beacon Press books are published under the auspices
of the Unitarian Universalist Association
Published simultaneously in hardcover and paperback editions
All rights reserved
Printed in the United States of America

9 8 7 6 5 4 3 2 1

The poems "Thank You — Come Again" and "Epigrams,"
copyright © 1967 by Ronald Gross, are reprinted by
permission of Simon and Schuster.
The quotation and illustration by Charles Amirkhanian on pages 115-116
are reprinted from *R.S.V.P. Cycles* by Lawrence Halprin,
copyright © 1969 by Lawrence Halprin, by permission
of the publisher, George Braziller, Inc.

Library of Congress Cataloging in Publication Data

Schrank, Jeffrey.
   Deception detection.
   Includes bibliographical references.
    1. Advertising — Psychological aspects.
2. Advertising — Social aspects — United States.
3. Nonverbal communication.   4. Perception.
I. Title.
HF5822.S287   659.1'07   75-5293
ISBN 0-8070-3160-7
ISBN 0-8070-3161-5 (pbk.)

Contents

1 Survival Skills in a Consumer Society: Deception in the Marketplace   1

    The critical evaluation of advertising claims — survival in the microcosmic world of the SUPERmarket — mass media and consumer deception — activities and resources.

2 Nonverbal Communication: Seeing Through Deception in Communication   36

    The language of gesture, space, and the environment. Activities and resources.

3 A Primer in Mind Management: Media Deception   63

    The educational content of entertainment programming — sex roles analysis — the message of television news — analysis worksheets for local papers and newscasts — propaganda as news — resource guide.

4 Creativity Training: Escaping the Deception That Logic is ALL   100

    Imitation — playing around — word play — generating alternatives — meditation on a bunch of grapes — brainstorming — creative projection — cliché consciousness — resources.

5 Visual Awareness   129

    SEEing the ordinary — shape consciousness — photoanalysis — creating visual surprises — kicking the habit of word addiction — facades — color awareness — changing vision — resources.

1

Survival Skills in a Consumer Society: Deception in the Marketplace

DVERTISING is not only an attempt to persuade; it is also education. Advertising is a constantly repeated course in how to behave in the marketplace. Viewed this way, a course in marketplace survivial is not optional; the only question is whether it will be taught by schools or by advertisers. To leave consumer education in the hands of advertisers is nearly as wise as having monkeys guard a banana plantation. But many school systems consider consumer eduation a peripheral option and fail to realize that if schools do not teach marketplace skills, advertisers will.

Advertising can succeed as education only in the absence of impartial consumer information representing the people's interests rather than the sellers'. The success of advertising (in today's form) is a measure of the failure of consumer education. For many years consumer education in schools languished; it had about as much status as basket-weaving and therapeutic woodworking. But today's schools are increasingly realizing that to teach students to survive in the marketplace requires a solid interdisciplinary course. The new status of what is usually called "consumer education" was helped by words of warning from scientists and researchers. Ralph Nader, Paul Ehrlich, Barry Commoner and others warned that our patterns of consumption would bring about the end of society as we know it sometime soon unless drastic changes took place. Add to these media-amplified warnings the rising prices that turned the relaxed atmosphere of supermarkets into one of hostile tension where shoppers exchanged whispered rumors that the express check-out lane was to be changed from "8 items or less" to "$50 or less." Emerging from all this was a new realization that coping with the world of sellers and buyers is an extremely crucial skill.

Consumer education can be viewed as a direct descendant of more primitive skills such as hunting, surviving in a jungle, raising crops, or building a shelter in the wilderness. Today's basic problems are the same, but the solutions far more abstract and complex. The old consumer skills have now become part craft and part counterculture status symbol. *The Whole Earth Catalog* is a consumer's guide and *Foxfire* is a form of consumer education manual — dated enough to be quaint rather than merely irrelevant.

Teaching someone how to build a log cabin or how to make yogurt is more exciting (or at least "different") than teaching the complexities of processed food deceptions or the ins and outs of misleading ads from banks and savings and loan associations. But for 205 million Americans learning to stalk wild asparagus is far less important than learning to stalk honest value for hard-earned money in the neon neatness of the grocery store.

This chapter is an introduction to teaching only a few of the many crucial skills needed to avoid marketplace deception. It is *not* an outline for a consumer education course; it is a collection of ideas that could be part of a consumer education course. It is also a collection of related ideas that could be studied in a unit on American problems, sociology, family living, home economics, language arts (especially the section on advertising and label interpretation), chemistry (processed food and additives) or many other electives. As with all chapters in this book, the ideas are specifically written with high school students in mind but could easily be used in junior high, college, or adult education with a few adaptations. The ideas here teach a few skills that are crucial both now and in the future. The skills included are:

- Coping with advertising claims.
- Survival in the microcosmic world of the supermarket.

- Understanding how the mass media contribute to consumer deception.

THE CRITICAL EVALUATION OF ADVERTISING CLAIMS

High school students, and many teachers, are notorious believers in their own immunity to advertising. These naive inhabitants of consumerland believe that advertising is childish, dumb, a bunch of lies, and influences only the vast hordes of the less sophisticated. Their own purchases, they think, are made purely on the basis of value and desire, with advertising playing only a minor supporting role. They know about Vance Packard and his "hidden persuaders" and the adman's psychosell and bag of persuasive magic. They are not impressed.

Advertisers know better. Although few people admit to being greatly influenced by ads, surveys and sales figures show that a well-designed advertising campaign has dramatic effects. A logical conclusion is that advertising works below the level of conscious awareness and it works even on those who claim immunity to its message. Ads are designed to have an effect while being laughed at, belittled, and all but ignored.

A person unaware of advertising's claim on him is precisely the one most vulnerable to the adman's attack. Advertisers delight in an audience that believes ads to be harmless nonsense, for such an audience is rendered defenseless by its belief that there is no attack taking place. The purpose of classroom study of advertising is to raise the level of awareness about the persuasive techniques used in ads. One way to do this is to analyze ads in microscopic detail. Ads can be studied to detect their psychological hooks, how they are used to gauge values and hidden desires of the common man. They can be studied for their use of symbols, color, and imagery. But perhaps the simplest and most direct way to study ads is through an analysis of the language of the advertising claim.

The "claim" is the verbal or print part of an ad that makes some claim of superiority for the product being advertised. After studying claims, students should be able to recognize those that are misleading and accept as useful information those that are true. A few of these claims are downright lies, some are honest statements about a truly superior product, but most fit into the category of neither bold lies nor helpful consumer information. They balance on the narrow line between truth and falsehood by a careful choice of words.

The reason so many ad claims fall into this category of pseudo-information is that they are applied to parity products, those in which all or most of the brands available are nearly identical. Since no one superior product exists, advertising is used to create the illusion of superiority. The largest advertising budgets are devoted to parity products such as gasoline, cigarettes, beer and soft drinks, soaps, and various headache and cold remedies.

The first rule of parity claims involves the Alice-in-Wonderland use of the words "better" and "best." In parity claims, "better" means "best" but "best" only means "equal to." If all the brands are identical, they must all be equally good, the legal minds have decided. So "best" means that the product is as good as the other superior products in its category. When Bing Crosby declares Minute Maid Orange Juice "the best there is," he means it is as good as the other orange juices you can buy.

The word "better," however, as grammarians will be pleased to hear, is legally as well as logically comparative and therefore becomes a clear claim to superiority. Bing could not have said that Minute Maid is "better than any other orange juice." "Better" is a claim to superiority. The only time "better" can be used is when a product does indeed have superiority over other products in its category or when the "better" is used to compare the product with something other than competing brands. An orange juice could therefore claim to be "better than a vitamin pill," or even that it was "the better breakfast drink."

The second rule of advertising-claim analysis is simply that if any product is truly superior, the ad will say so very clearly and will offer some kind of convincing evidence of the superiority. If an ad hedges the least about a product's advantage over the competition, you can strongly suspect it is not superior — maybe equal to but not better. You will never hear a gasoline company say, "We will give you four miles per gallon more in your car than any other brand." They would love to make such a claim, but it would not be true. Gasoline is a parity product, and, in spite of some very clever and deceptive ads of a few years ago, no one has yet claimed one brand of gasoline better than — and therefore superior to — any other brand.

To create the necessary illusion of superiority, advertisers usually re-

Survival Skills in a Consumer Society

sort to one or more of the following ten basic techniques. Each is common and easy to identify.

1. The Weasel Claim

A weasel word is a modifier that practically negates the claim that follows. The expression "weasel word" is aptly named after the egg-eating habits of weasels. A weasel will suck out the inside of an egg, leaving it to appear intact to the casual observer. Upon closer examination, the egg is discovered to be hollow. Words or claims that appear substantial upon first glance but disintegrate into hollow meaninglessness on analysis are weasels. Commonly used weasel words include "helps" (the champion weasel), "like" (used in a comparative sense), "virtual" or "virtually," "acts" or "works," "can be," "up to," "as much as," "refreshes," "comforts," "tackles," "fights," "comes on," "the feel of," "the look of," "looks like," "fortified," "enriched," and "strengthened."

Samples of Weasel Claims

"Helps control dandruff symptoms with regular use."
The weasels include "helps control," and possibly even "symptoms," and "regular use." The claim is not "stops dandruff."

"Leaves dishes *virtually* spotless"
We have seen so many ad claims that we have learned to tune out weasels. You are supposed to think "spotless," rather than "virtually" spotless.

"Only half the price of *many* color sets"
"Many "is the weasel. The claim is supposed to give the impression that the set is inexpensive.

"Tests confirm one mouthwash *best* against mouth odor."
"Hot Nestles' cocoa is the very *best*."
Remember the "best" and "better" routine.

"Listerine *fights* bad breath."
"Fights," not "stops."

"Lots of things have changed, but Hershey's *goodness* hasn't."
The claim does not say that Hershey's chocolate hasn't changed.

"Bacos, the crispy garnish that *tastes* just *like* its name."

2. The Unfinished Claim

The unfinished claim is one in which the ad claims the product is better, or has more of something but does not finish the comparison.

Samples of Unfinished Claims

"Magnavox gives you more."

More what?

"Anacin: Twice as much of the pain reliever doctors recommend most."

This claim fits in a number of categories; as an unfinished claim it does not say twice as much of what pain reliever.

"Supergloss does it with more color, more shine, more sizzle, more!"

"Coffee-mate gives coffee more body, more flavor."

Also note that "body" and "flavor" are weasels.

"You can be sure if it's Westinghouse."

Sure of what?

"Scott makes it better for you."

Makes what better? How is it better?

"Ford LTD — 700% quieter."

When the Federal Trade Commission asked Ford to substantiate this claim, Ford revealed that they meant the inside of the Ford was seven hundred percent quieter than the outside.

3. The "We're Different and Unique" Claim

This kind of claim states simply that there is nothing else quite like the product advertised. For example, if Schlitz were to add pink food coloring to their beer, they could say, "There's nothing like new pink Schlitz." The uniqueness claim is supposed to be interpreted by readers as a claim to superiority.

Samples of "We're Different and Unique" Claims

"There's no other mascara like it."

"Only Doral has this unique filter system."
"Cougar is like nobody else's car."
"Either way, liquid or spray, there's nothing else like it."
"If it doesn't say Goodyear, it can't be Polyglas."

"Polyglas" is a trade name copyrighted by Goodyear. Goodrich or Firestone could make a tire exactly identical to the Goodyear one and yet couldn't call it "Polyglas" — a name for fiberglass belts.

'Only Zenith has Chromacolor."

Same as the "Polyglas" gambit. Admiral has Solarcolor and RCA has Accucolor.

4. The "Water Is Wet" Claim

"Water is wet" claims say something about the product that is true for any brand in that product category (e.g. "Schrank's water is really wet"). The claim is usually a statement of fact, but not a real advantage over the competition.

Samples of "Water Is Wet" Claims

"Mobil: the Detergent Gasoline"

Any gasoline acts as a cleaning agent.

"Great Lash greatly increases the diameter of every lash."
"Rheingold: the natural beer"

Made from grains and water as are other beers.

"SKIN smells differently on everyone."

As do many perfumes.

5. The "So What" Claim

This is the kind of claim to which the careful reader will react by saying, "So what?" A claim is made that is true but gives no real advantage to the product. This is similar to the "water is wet" claim except that it claims an advantage that is not shared by most of the other brands in the product category.

Samples of "So What" Claims

"Geritol has more than twice the iron of ordinary supplements."

But is it twice as beneficial to the body?

"Campbell's gives you tasty pieces of chicken and not one but two chicken stocks."

Does the presence of two stocks improve the taste?

"Strong enough for a man but made for a woman"

This deodorant claim says only that the product is aimed at the female market.

6. The Vague Claim

The vague claim is simply not clear. This category often overlaps with others. The key to the vague claim is the use of words that are colorful but meaningless, as well as the use of subjective and emotional opinions that defy verification. Most contain weasels.

Samples of Vague Claims

"Lips have never looked so luscious."

Can you imagine trying to either prove or disprove such a claim?

"Lipsavers are fun — they taste good, smell good and feel good."

"Its deep rich lather makes hair feel new again."

"For skin like peaches and cream"

"The end of meatloaf boredom"

"Take a bite and you'll think you're eating on the Champs Elysées."

"Winston tastes good like a cigarette should."

The perfect little portable for all-around viewing with all the features of higher-priced sets"

"Fleischmann's makes sensible eating delicious."

7. The Endorsement or Testimonial

A celebrity or authority appears in an ad to lend his or her stellar qualities to the product. Sometimes the people will actually claim to use the product, but very often they don't. There are agencies surviving on providing products with testimonials.

Samples of Endorsements or Testimonials

"Joan Fontaine throws a shot-in-the-dark party and her friends learn a thing or two."

"Darling, have you discovered Masterpiece? The most exciting men I know are smoking it." (Eva Gabor)

"Vega is the best handling car ever made in the U.S."

This claim was challenged by the FTC, but GM answered that the claim is only a direct quote from *Road and Track* magazine.

8. The Scientific or Statistical Claim

This kind of ad uses some sort of scientific proof or experiment, very specific numbers, or an impressive-sounding mystery ingredient.

Samples of Scientific or Statistical Claims

"Wonder Bread helps build strong bodies 12 ways."

Even the weasel "helps" did not prevent the FTC from demanding this ad be withdrawn. But note that the use of the number "12" makes the claim far more believable than if it were taken out.

"Easy-Off has 33% more cleaning power than another popular brand."

"Another popular brand" often translates as some other kind of oven cleaner sold somewhere. Also, the claim does not say Easy-Off works thirty-three percent better.

"Special Morning — 33% more nutrition"

Also an unfinished claim.

"Certs contains a sparkling drop of Retsyn."

"ESSO with HTA"

"Sinarest. Created by a research scientist who actually gets sinus headaches."

9. The "Compliment the Consumer" Claim

This kind of claim butters up the consumer by some form of flattery.

Samples of "Compliment the Consumer Claims"

"If you do what is right for you, no matter what others do, then RC Cola is right for you."
"We think a cigar smoker is someone special."
"You pride yourself on your good home cooking . . . ."
"The lady has taste."
"You've come a long way baby."

10. The Rhetorical Question

This technique demands a response from the audience. A question is asked and the viewer or listener is supposed to answer in such a way as to affirm the product's goodness.

Samples of Rhetorical Questions

"Plymouth — isn't that the kind of car America wants?"
"Shouldn't your family be drinking Hawaiian Punch?"
"What do you want most from coffee? That's what you get most from Hills."
"Touch of Sweden: could your hands use a small miracle?"

SURVIVAL IN THE SUPERMARKET

The supermarket is to modern man what the jungle was to primitive people. It is the source of food that has to be sought out with great skill in order to obtain the best quality. Economic traps and threats camouflaged as harmless goodies lurk in every aisle. Shopping, like hunting, is a game of skill with survival as the prize.

In the supermarket the shopper matches wits with big business, advertising, marketing, and packaging in all its splendor and subtleties. Let us consider the supermarket as a kind of combination jungle/battleground. For the shopper to emerge victorious (and the odds are against this since the battle is always fought on the enemy's territory) he or she has to purchase the most nutritious, best-tasting food for the least amount of money. The food manufacturers win (and the store shares in the victory) if the shopper buys more than is needed or desired, or spends a fair percentage of the total on high-priced products that contain little food value.

The shopper's only defensive tactic is knowledge. A course in consumer survival has to do more than teach about eating a good breakfast and mixing green and yellow vegetables. In fact, shopping cannot be left to the nutrition teacher; it is part economics, part chemistry, part critical thinking, and part reading skill.

The kind of knowledge needed to survive in the supermarket game is not, as we have seen, provided by advertising. Yet, when one is out of school, advertising is the prime source of consumer education, teaching you how to minister to your body, stomach, and soul. In fact, advertising contributes to deception not only by failing to provide useful information, but also by helping to obscure the identities of the food manufacturers.

The Brand Name Deception

Everyone old enough to watch television knows the Jolly Green Giant is a benevolent master, that Betty Crocker is a nice old lady who cooks as Grandma used to, and that Sara Lee bakes cakes that "nobody doesn't like." But how many users of these products know who is the maker behind the brand name? Ignorance of the company behind the brand makes judging new products difficult, makes it difficult to register either complaints or praise, and gives shoppers the illusion of variety. For when all the brand names are matched with their corporate owners, it becomes clear that a handful of companies exercise control over supermarket selection.

Here's a test to take and use in a classroom to illustrate that corporate makers hide behind brand images. Match the product on the left with the corporation on the right who makes that product.

1. Betty Crocker
2. Mad Magazine
3. Smith Brothers cough drops
4. Chiquita bananas and lettuce
5. Ultra Ban anti-perspirant
6. Ultra Brite toothpaste

A. Gillette Company
B. General Mills
C. Colgate-Palmolive
D. Warner-Lambert
E. Procter & Gamble
F. Warner Communications

7. Schick safety razors
8. Welcome Wagon
9. A & W Root Beer
10. Sure anti-perspirant
11. Flair pens
12. Secret anti-perspirant
13. Hamburger Helper

G. United Brands
H. Bristol-Myers
I. Right Guard, Incorporated

Answers to brand matching test:

1 – B	5 – H	8 – A	11 – A
2 – F	6 – C	9 – G	12 – E
3 – D	7 – D	10 – E	13 – B
4 – G			

Note that 1 and 13 are the same, as are 3 and 7, 4 and 9, 8 and 11, and 10 and 12.

To give a better idea of how a large food corporation presents the illusion of variety while limiting the number of truly competing brands, here are brands owned by three large companies who make the things that fill supermarket shelves.

Consolidated Foods owns the companies who produce B an' G pickles, Booth's Ocean Seafoods, Bryan Brothers meats, Chicken Delight, Hollywood Candy, Hickory Grove meats, Sara Lee, Azar Nuts, Idaho Frozen Foods, Lawson milk, Monarch Institutional Foods, Popsicle, Shasta beverages. All these in addition to Sirena swimwear, Abbey Furniture Rentals, Electrolux vacuum cleaners, Fuller Brushes, and more.

Unilever (a conglomerate that includes Lever Brothers and Lipton among others) is the power behind Golden Glow, Good Luck, Imperial, and Promise margarines; Butterworth's syrups; Lucky Whip; Spry Shortening; Aim, Close-up, Pepsodent, Stripe, and Twice as Nice toothpastes, All, Breeze, Caress, Dove, Drive, Final Touch, Handy Andy, Lifebouy, Lux, Phase III, Praise, Rinso, Silver Dust, Surf, Swan and Wisk cleaning products; Lipton's tea; Wish-Bone dressings; Good Humor ice cream; Tabby Treat and Total Dinners pet foods.

General Foods is the company behind Bird's Eye, Awake, Cool 'n Creamy, Cool Whip, Great Shakes, Iceflow Slush, Orange Plus, Quick Thaw, Thick and Frosty, Burger Chef, Burpee seeds, Jell-O, D-Zerta, Dream Whip, Minute Rice, Sure-Jell, Kool-Aid, Good Seasons, Open

Pit, Shake 'n Bake, Swan's Down, Toast 'em, Twist, Maxwell House, Brim, Maxim, Sanka, Yuban, Alpha-Bits, Post Raisin Bran, Post Grape-Nuts, Post Toasties, Postum, Sugar Crisp, Log Cabin, Start, Tang, Gainesburgers, Gravy Train, Prime, Top Choice and Viviane Woodward cosmetics.

Ingredients Deception

That the average shopper does not know WHO he or she is buying from is bad enough, but even worse is that so many people don't know WHAT they are buying. When food was something caught the week before or grown in the fields behind the house, the eater knew the history of the food. But when food becomes something sold in stores and produced in rarely seen processing plants, eater's alienation sets in. The eater knows the cost of the food but has only a vague idea of what it contains. This lack of knowledge about ingredients enables corporations to sell inexpensive food at higher prices.

Some new products from General Foods serve nicely to illustrate how food manufacturers take advantage of ingredients ignorance. General Foods is marketing instant "gourmet" coffees under the names Café au Lait, Cafe Vienna and Suisse Mocha. They are soluble ("instant") coffee with a bit of artificial milk (Café au Lait and Vienna) or chocolate (Suisse Mocha) flavoring. Café au Lait sells for $2.78 a pound and is nothing more than instant coffee with loads of non-dairy creamer, a bit of sugar, and artificial flavoring. In spite of the addition of cheap non-dairy creamer powder as the main ingredient (there is more non-dairy creamer in the can than coffee) the cost is three times as much per serving as one-hundred percent coffee. Now, how many people would willingly pay General Foods three times as much for a cup of coffee just to save the trouble of stirring in their own creamer and sugar? Since the product is sold as "the coffee the French drink" and potential purchasers have learned to read the ads on the labels instead of the list of ingredients, the products might succeed. GF hopes their "International Coffees" line will capture three to four percent of the $700-million soluble coffee market.

New food research seeks to turn cheap non-foods into desirable and expensive food. The main difference between new food research and ancient alchemy is that food engineers have succeeded where alchemists failed. Often no real scientific innovation is needed, only the marketing man's inspiration of combining two or more ordinary food items into a new and expensive "gourmet treat." One such innovation now in the supermarket is a twenty-six-dollars-a-pound instant coffee. The secret discovered by a small coffee company was to mix a touch of anise and dextrose (sugar substitute) with the coffee, a move which costs little but enables them to sell the result as "Cafe Anisette" in small foil packages as a gourmet item. In this way, .42 ounce sells for 69¢ – $26.28 a pound.

The food alchemist's favorite building block is the soybean. In Japan soybean "cakes" are nearly a dietary staple. They are inexpensive, nutritious, and high in protein. In the United States soybeans are controlled by the large food companies and are not sold as a source of inexpensive protein. Instead they become the food alchemist's magic ingredient. "Textured soy protein" is disguised to look and taste like bacon chips and sells for $4.06 a pound. Or it is done up as "Country Cuts" to imitate chicken and ham or sold as All American Fun-Links aping the ever popular hot dog. Soy substitutes for meat make economic, nutritional, and ecological sense, but to disguise the soy as a more expensive product and then sell it at a price slightly less than that for which it substitutes smacks of the alchemy factor instead of concern for human beings.

The food shopper has one major defense against marketing alchemy and that is a solid grasp of the art of reading ingredients lists on packages. A skilled label reader would immediately have recognized Café au Lait for the marketing ploy it is and would have considered Cafe Anisette as something to try at home by adding anise from the spice rack to ordinary instant coffee.

A shopper out to buy a quick can of chili is faced, let us say, with three varieties. A person who does not read labels may buy the can with the best picture on the label or the most familiar advertised brand. But the label-wise shopper immediately reads the fine print. Strangely enough each can contains 15 ounces (no doubt it was once an even pound) and sells for 59¢ – coincidence no doubt. Two of the three are produced by conglomerates a close reading of the tiny print reveals – Broadcast from United Brands and Chef Boy Ar Dee from

American Home Foods. The labels so far have given no clue to value. A glance at the contents of each can reveals that two of the three have water as the main ingredient. The third has beans, beef, tomatoes and then water for contents — clearly the most food for the money. One of the watery brands, however, is the only one that does not contain modified food starch as a thickener (it uses cereal instead) and this might sway the choice of the ingredient-wise shopper.

Over in a different aisle the same careful shopper notices Kraft Sandwich Spread has some jars with new ingredients and some with the familiar list. The change removes mayonnaise from the sandwich spread and substitutes soybean oil — the price remains the same. The shopper decides to mix his or her own pickle relish and mayonnaise instead of hiring Kraft to perform that simple function.

This shopper has learned from looking at labels and prices that the more processed a food, the more it is sold as a "convenience item," the less food value it contains. Convenience foods often provide very little convenience and are best left for people who want to hire large corporations to mix food ingredients at a high cost, according to a corporate recipe. The shopper who spends one or two hours clipping coupons and shuffling to various stores for specials in order to buy overpriced convenience is a sad example of ingredients ignorance.

The area of the supermarket where ingredient deception is even more prevalent than in the food section is drugs and cosmetics. Very few people have the slightest idea of the contents or even the efficacy of mouthwash, toothpaste, various pain remedies, and cosmetics. Health education has been taken over by the advertising industry through ads for various drug companies. Americans believe that bowels must move with the regularity of a military drill and at least once a day, that headaches are caused by noisy children (ads never teach that people cause their own headaches), that tension can be relieved by pills, that the sins of overeating can be erased by various liquids, that mouthwashes prevent colds and there are pills that cure a cold. The fact that there is no medical evidence to support these claims (and there is plenty to suggest that they are not only false but dangerous) does not reach the masses. All this ad education leads average Americans to take sedatives and stimulants to the tune of well over one hundred single dosage pills yearly, to spend $280 million a year for mouthwashes known to be no more useful than water and to spend about $200 a gallon for nose drops that cost only $10 or less a gallon to make.

Americans will spend three to ten times more for a heavily advertised "brand name" than its identical counterpart in a less well-known brand.

Knowledge of the most common ingredients in food and drug items is an essential part of the equipment needed to win the supermarket game. The activities at the end of this chapter suggest some ways to begin. The print resources list tells where to find the needed information. Such knowledge has to be taught in schools since neither advertising nor the mass media have deemed such information worthy of the public good.

MASS MEDIA AND CONSUMER DECEPTION

Ignorance about corporate food producers and a general lack of knowledge about what food contains and its nutritional value can be laid partly to advertising, partly to the failure of schools to counter the biased education of advertising, and partly to the mass media. Television, newspapers, and magazines certainly could provide the shopper with useful information to help counter advertising bias, but the advertisers pay the bills of the media and the result is a constriction, if not almost total absence, of useful consumer information. A few examples of media failings paint a disappointing picture.

On national television (and in purely statistical terms national television is the only true MASS medium we have) consumer issues are rarely mentioned in newscasts, but they are even less apt to be treated in an in-depth documentary. When NBC televised a program about the sad condition of migrant workers, Coca-Cola moved $1 million of its advertising to competing networks. Some of the filthiest and most dilapidated migrant camps shown in the documentary were owned by Coca-Cola's Minute Maid division. Coke, of course, denied that the sudden switch in ad money had anything to do with the unfavorable publicity in the documentary. But the message of their action was a clear "let the broadcaster beware." But broadcasters and news outlet owners seldom have to be reminded of their own dependence on advertising revenue.

When the FTC charged Sears, the nation's largest retailer, with bait-and-switch sales tactics only the *Washington Post* considered the item front-page news. CBS-TV included the story in its evening news while ABC and NBC did not consider it worthy of even a passing mention. Most newspapers carried the story, but very few attempted to localize it or to explain the workings of a "bait and switch" sales pitch.

Except for announcements of food poisoning and some auto recalls, the three networks do little consumer education as part of their news. Logs of the three network evening news shows reveal that in January of 1972 ABC offered only 9 items of consumer interest, CBS gave 10 and NBC 17. Of the combined 36 stories only 5 lasted as long as 3 minutes and half were under 20 seconds. According to a talk by Arthur Rowse, editor of *Consumer Newsweek,* an incomplete list of stories ignored that month by the networks included: the recall of 3 million cans of Coca-Cola, Sprite and Fanta drinks; the recall of 30,000 General Motors cars for collapsing wheels; an FTC consent order requiring Procter and Gamble to stop claiming that foods cooked in Crisco were less greasy and lower in calories; a government report that 88,900 highway bridges were "critically deficient" in safety aspects; an estimate by Senator William Proxmire that credit life insurance overcharges amount to $454 million a year; and the recall of 200,000 soup bowls distributed by Campbell Soup Company for exceeding maximum levels for toxic lead and cadmium.

It is hard to believe that only coincidence governs the fact that all of the companies missed in these stories were among the top fifty television advertisers that year.

Even ad-free public television has problems. Local NET stations sometimes refuse to carry critical programs, such as the in-depth look at how banks rob people, "Banks and The Poor," and a Detroit station blacked out a documentary unfavorable to the institution of the automobile.

Newspapers in some cities are beginning to name names and give solid consumer information, but deception is still the name of the ruling game for most readers. The FTC accused A & P of misleading advertising — a substantial number of sale items (20%) were either not available or were priced higher than the advertised price. Newspapers reacted to the story cautiously even though the story affects millions of shoppers. Freelance writer Jean Synder surveyed papers in Atlanta, Chicago, Durham, Milwaukee, and Raleigh and found that eight out of twelve failed even to report the story. This failure was in spite of a 500-word wire-service item that could have been widely used.

In Chicago, where only one paper covered the FTC charges, other press-release stories from food chains appeared three times in the following days. A & P is, of course, one of the nation's largest newspaper advertisers.

Another story further illustrates media's failure to inform consumers. *Christian Science Monitor* news service distributed a one-page story that included the sound consumer advice to "shop-once-a-week." One newspaper editor who ran the money-saving advice found that both the publisher and advertisers objected and had the story removed by the next edition. In order to test his judgment the editor of that paper surveyed 25 publishers and 25 editors of newspapers in the 25,000 - 100,000 circulation range at a publishers' convention. He found that only 16 percent would allow that advice to be published. Most of those who said they would not run such advice felt it amounted to biting the hand that feeds.

News about the supermarket is controlled by the fact that food stores account for a large percentage of newspaper revenues. National media are also supported by a handful of large corporations who control the food industry. The consumer is kept behind a veil of deception not because of some grand conspiracy, but simply because the news media, although intended to serve the buyers, are supported by the sellers.

ACTIVITIES TO COMBAT DECEPTION IN THE MARKETPLACE

The overall message of these activities is that the buyer does indeed have to beware but that with a bit of study caution will be rewarded. All of these activities are designed to be shared in a classroom. They can be adapted to almost any level of schooling from a graduate course in marketing to a high school consumer education course, or in teaching younger students some of the economic facts of life.

Activities for Evaluating Advertising Claims

1. Collect, categorize, and analyze advertising claims according to the

Survival Skills in a Consumer Society

ten techniques presented in this chapter. Remember that there may be other types of claims and that some are difficult to classify completely in any one category. Look for advertising claims that fit category 11 — honest and useful consumer information.

2. Compare product claims with the product performance. Construct a series of tests to verify the claims made about a particular product.

3. Rewrite ad claims so they give information that would help a customer make a wise buying decision. Write honest ads you consider misleading.

4. Write manufacturers and ask them to back up the claims they present in their corporate advertising. A college class in marketing tried this and found that many companies did not respond and very few took up the challenge. Addresses can be found in the *TV Sponsors Product Directory* (see "Print Resources" at the end of this chapter).

5. Find the emotional hooks in ads. This would include appeals to status, security, acceptance, patriotism, happiness, etc. Vance Packard is still a most useful source of ideas.

6. Select some parity product and write advertising claims for it, illustrating each of the ten techniques explained in this chapter. For example, if you select a mousetrap as your parity product (not the "better" mousetrap, just an ordinary one) your ad claims might include:

- Weasel — "Often helps control your rodent problem"
- Unfinished — "Kills rats better and faster"
- We're unique — "Only Imperial mousetraps have that unique Imperial craftsmanship behind them."
- Water is wet — "Spring action mousetrap"
- So what? — "Make with the finest knotty pine and tempered steel. Uses any kind of cheese as bait and comes in a variety of sizes."
- Vague claim — "Imperial mousetraps are easy to operate, effective, and can make you feel like a new person again without that annoying fear of being eaten alive by a hungry mouse."
- Endorsement — "None of my friends will ever go near an Imperial mousetrap. Believe me." — Mickey Mouse
- Scientific claim — "Works 33% faster than another popular brand under normal conditions."

- Compliment   "For the man whose time is too important to spend hunting mice."
- Rhetorical question   "Shouldn't your family have the feeling of Imperial safety?"

7. Attempt to reconstruct advertising demonstrations shown on television and make conclusions from your results. Write the companies concerned and tell them about your experiments. One class decided to test STP's claim that it is more slippery than oil. The class found that it could hold an oil-dipped screwdriver by the blade end but could not hold an STP-dipped tool. The class concluded that the STP claim was honest, and told STP of their results. The entire class was featured in the television spot for STP as a sort of unsolicited endorsement. The class forgot, however, that STP is not sold to prevent people from picking up screwdrivers; their test was totally irrelevant to the real function of the product. Beware of "red herring" tests and demonstrations in your own explorations.

Activities to Seek out Deception in the Supermarket

1. Have each student conduct a survey of the home cupboard or pantry. The survey should note each canned or packaged item in the house food supply and the manufacturer of the item. This inventory will familiarize students with the larger corporations and will demonstrate corporate control.

2. Obtain a classroom copy of the *Television Sponsors Product Directory*. The book is a must for any course about advertising or consumer education. It lists brand names and tells which company makes that brand. It also lists corporations and the various brands they distribute. Also provided are addresses of corporation board chairpersons, and state consumer offices. The 200-plus page paperback lists over 4,000 products. Available in quarterly subscriptions or single copies from Everglades Publishing Company, P.O. Drawer Q, Everglades, Florida 33929.

3. One area in which brand-name worship costs consumers millions of dollars yearly is in over-the-counter and prescription drugs. Have students research the concept of saving money by purchasing unadvertised over-the-counter drugs and by having doctors write prescrip-

tions generically instead of by brand name. Useful books for this research include *Handbook of Non-Prescription Drugs, Hot War on the Consumer,* and *The Medicine Show.*

4. Write for the annual reports of the nation's larger food manufacturers and make these available to the class. Some public libraries have annual reports on file. Companies will send such reports to interested investors and individuals.

5. Investigate the food sold in your school, especially via machines. Does the presence of vending machines that dispense "junk food" in schools in any way constitute education, or endorsement of such food? One mother in Indiana noticed that her children would not eat their lunches, preferring instead candy and snack foods from school vending machines. She learned that in one school day the 530 children drank 500 soft drinks and consumed 300 candy bars. She campaigned to have junk-food machines removed, but was opposed by school officials who saw the machines as a source of needed revenue. She finally won her battle; as one school board member commented, "We should reject any system that profits from the poor nutritional habits of our teenagers." What is the status of junk food at your school?

6. Prepare an "Honesty-in-Labeling" list. This list would name foods according to their true ingredients. For example, a frozen "Spinach Soufflé" that contains more skim milk than spinach is renamed "Skim Milk Soufflé," or dried instant noodle soup that contains salt as its main ingredient becomes "Noodle Flavored Salt Soup," while many brands of Chili can be accurately renamed "Water and Beef with Beans." A frozen "Polynesian Style Dinner" becomes after a careful reading of the fine print, a "Rehydrated Potato Flake Dinner."

7. Find the various euphemisms and sound-alike words used by the food industry that might deceive consumers. A few examples would include crème for cream, whitener, strawberry flavor pie (as opposed to strawberry pie), Bacos, or blueberry-like muffins.

8. Do some comparative taste-testing among various brands of the same processed food. Compare the same food in its processed version with its un- (or less) processed version.

9. Devise some experiments to measure accurately the quantities of various ingredients in processed foods. Also compare the picture on the label with the reality inside.

10. Analyze your own diet in terms of the system presented in *Nutrition Scoreboard* (see "Print Resources").

11. Extend your research to the food served in restaurants. For example, prepare a consumer's guide to the local fast-food franchises.

12. Prepare a price-per-pound list of various processed foods to determine true value. Compare the price of a convenience food that contains, for example, noodles and tuna with the price of noodles and tuna bought separately. Determine how much time, if any, the prepackaged items saves. Such research will often convince even a pseudo-food addict that much food is both overpriced and undeserving of the name "convenience food."

13. Prepare a "handy pocket guide to the most often used additives." The resulting publication could be made available to shoppers in the area either by sale or free distribution. *The Eater's Digest* (see "Print Resources") is a helpful reference for this project. One of the goals of the food unit could be to teach basic label reading. Students should certainly know that ingredients are listed on labels in descending order of quantity — the first listed ingredient is the one present in the largest quantity, the last listed ingredient is that present in the smallest quantity.

14. Use ingredients lists to find products that are identical yet compete with each other or are sold by the same company under different names. Begin with cleaning agents, cereals, medicines, and imitation products. Compare prices.

15. Learn about standards of identity for those products that do not have ingredients listed on the label. For example, ice-cream manufacturers need not list ingredients on the container. The contents of the package determines its identity. A package labeled vanilla ice cream is different from vanilla-flavored ice cream; and both are different from artificially flavored vanilla ice cream.

16. Study advertised claims made for drugs sold over the counter.

If there is a field office of the FTC in your area, contact them and ask if the results of the "advertising claim substantiation program" are available to the public. The FTC has asked manufacturers to prove their advertising claims on a few products: the proofs submitted by the manufacturers are available for research at the FTC offices.

One FTC study found that cough and cold remedies all use essentially the same generic ingredients, the manufacturers do little or no clinical research, rely largely on standard medical texts for scientific support, and differ mostly in the proportions of ingredients and the words used in advertising.

For example, Vicks 4-Way Nasal Spray claims in an ad that it "contains more kinds of decongestant — more than any leading nasal spray." In reply to the FTC, Bristol-Myers, the makers of Vicks, said "no claims are made for 4-Way Nasal Spray as to superiority over the three leading sprays."

Students or teachers who are skeptical about the advertising section of this chapter would soon become true believers after even a casual study of the data gathered by the FTC.

Activities for Mass Media and Consumer Deception

1. Evaluate the food, business and real estate, and travel sections of your local paper. Are they mainly a collection of press releases and disguised advertising or a solid collection of useful consumer information?

2. Subscribe for the school library or class to *Media & Consumer* or obtain at least one issue for everyone in the class. See details in the "Print Resources" section, which follows.

RESOURCE GUIDE

Print Resources

Periodicals

Media & Consumer (P.O. Box 111, Uxbridge, MA 01569) is the single most useful periodical for students of marketplace deception. The monthly publication presents news of consumer interest and examples of the best consumer investigations published around the country. The paper does not test specific products or make purchasing recommendations; it is more concerned with whistle-blowing and with taking the pulse of the media's concern with the consumer.

Classroom quantities are available and would provide excellent material for discussion and further study.

Advertising Age (740 Rush Street, Chicago, IL 60611) is *the* trade journal of the advertising industry. Unlike many self-congratulatory industry trade journals, *Advertising Age* presents the conflicts within the worlds of advertising and marketing. The publication criticizes ads (a weekly "ads we can do without" spotlights the worst) and features excellent surveys on an industry-by-industry basis. *Advertising Age* is fascinating to read and gives a behind-the-scenes look at the attempts of advertisers both to serve the public and deceive it. Highly recommended for libraries or consumer courses.

Books About Advertising

There have been many books written by admen about the industry, but most of these seem aimed at fellow advertisers. The books described here (all available in paperback) are among the most critical and best written:

I Can Sell You Anything by Paul Stevens (Peter Weyden) is aptly subtitled "How I Made Your Favorite TV Commerical With Minimum Truth and Maximum Consequences." The book is usable for student reading in spite of the sloppy writing and almost nonexistent research. Stevens manages to draw on his own vast experience as an ad copywriter to explain how claims in ads are made to sound as if they promise the world, when, in fact, they merely declare it to be more round than square. The book changed my approach to advertising and enables readers to distinguish the phony ads from those which announce a superior product. The classification of the claims in this article is partly based on Stevens' ideas. *I Can Sell You Anything* is especially good in communications units, since it concentrates not on the emotional or or psychological manipulation but on the very careful wording of ads. Thousands of examples, fifth-grade reading level, and an eye-opener. Far from perfect, but for students very likely the best book on advertising currently available.

The Hidden Persuaders by Vance Packard (Pocket Books) is practically a classic and still usable despite its age. Packard's look at the emotional and motivational side of ads is a nice contrast and supplement to Wrighter's linguistic approach.

Down the Tube by Terry Galanoy (Pinnacle Books) is an "adman's behind-the-scenes tour of the making of commercials" book. *Down the Tube* relies heavily on anecdotes about the making of TV commercials. Certainly not as instructive as either Wrighter or Packard but fun to read and with redeeming social value. A fascinating glimpse into the world of television commercials.

The Permissible Lie: The Inside Truth About Advertising by Samm Sinclair Baker (Beacon Press) tells how ads distort the truth, yet it defends the institution of advertising. The book is dated but more comprehensive than *I Can Sell You Anything*. Baker devotes chapters to advertising research, program ratings, government regulation, and even to how to improve what you don't like and how to get the full value from your purchases.

Subliminal Seduction by Wilson Bryan Key (New American Library) is an outrageous book that could serve as the basis for one or more fascinating classes on advertising values.

Remember a few years back when some movie houses experimented with flashing subliminal messages like "eat popcorn" on the screen so fast they were registered by the eye but not consciously noticed? Angry editorials decried the new technique as an "insidious threat to our right to privacy." The messages reportedly did have some effect on audiences, but the technique quietly faded from public attention. But subliminal advertising is still very much alive, according to Key. His thesis is that subliminal advertising "embeds" and symbolism has been used secretly in magazines and TV ads for the past fifteen years.

Key says that thousands of ads in major magazines have the word "sex" and four-letter words secretly embedded in ice cubes, shadows, and backgrounds. A Hilton Hotel room-service menu has "sex" embedded from breakfast through dinner, "sex's" saturate the paper cover of Eldridge Cleaver's *Soul on Ice* and even the Sears' Catalog is loaded with "fascinating subliminal perversities."

In *Subliminal Seduction,* Key tries to blow the cover on the secret use of subliminal techniques designed to influence readers below the level of awareness. Not only are words camouflaged in ads, but symbols are used with the skill of a Freudian poet. "Commonly used phallic symbolism includes neckties, arrows, flagpoles, automobiles, rockets, pencils, cigars and cigarettes . . . the list is endless." Key finds full-page color ads (especially for liquor and cigarettes) in major magazines filled with hidden words and sexual symbolism.

To accept all of Key's book requires a highly active imagination and complete suspension of disbelief. The book contains numerous examples: some prove Key frighteningly correct, while others seem little better than interpretations by a college freshman who has just discovered a dictionary of symbolism. But Key's analysis is provocative, never dull, and does serve to alert readers to the fact that magazine ads have quite a bit going on that is missed on a conscious level by ninety-nine percent of their viewers.

Key is at his best in interpreting magazine covers as subconsciously seductive advertising for newsstand sales of the publication. He sees a number of *Playboy* covers symbolizing castration and a nursing mother. He similarly analyzes *Cosmopolitan* and *Vogue* as advertising pieces playing to the needs and desires of their intended audiences.

In spite of occasional brilliance, Key is carried away with his own theory. A true believer of *Subliminal Seduction* is probably someone who is also convinced that Beatle Paul McCartney is dead and that Marilyn Monroe was killed by the CIA.

It is difficult to read *Subliminal Seduction* with an open mind and not gain at least an increased awareness of advertising symbolism. A class presentation, complete with slides of some subliminal embeds, is never dull and usually provokes a far-reaching consideration of advertising values.

Books About the Supermarket Game

The Television Sponsors Product Directory (from Everglades Publishing Company, Everglades, FL 33929) is an essential reference book for any student of the corporate world of advertising in the marketplace.

The American Connection by John Pekkanen (Follett, 1973) is a highly critical look at the drug industry's attempt to turn us into a nation of pill-poppers. Pekkanen shows how amphetamines and barbiturates have been promoted as part of the American way of life and how their use by parents has led to abuse by children.

Consumer Beware by Beatrice Trim Hunter (Bantam) is the kind of book that could convert readers to organic eating. Hunter calls the search for new pseudo-foods "the race between toxicologist and undertaker." She is especially perceptive in dealing with the pollution of natural foods.

The Eater's Digest: The Consumer's Factbook of Food Additives by Michael Jacobson (Doubleday Anchor paperback, 1972) is the best single popular work on food additives. His section on food standards of identity and his dictionary of food additives are valuable additions to any reference library. This book is the most useful in translating labels of processed food.

The Foodbook by James Trager (Avon paperback) is a fascinating book about food. Trager is no health-food nut; rather he is a historian concerned with why we eat what we do. He knows that "While most of the world is forced to live on monotonously limited diets, the scope of our own diets is limited by stale habit and familiarity. Our store of food information is full of false facts." *The Foodbook* explores the sources of food and the roots of our eating patterns, our food taboos and myths, the techniques of producing and preserving food, and the modern additives used. This 575-page tome is great entertainment yet important education as well.

Food Pollution: The Violation of Our Inner Biology by Gene Marine and Judith Van Allen (Holt, Rinehart & Winston, 1971) is an indictment of the food processing industry. The book's theme is that "just as we have violated our outer ecology with DDT and untreated sewage and automobile exhaust, so are we violating our inner ecology; for we have gimmicked and tortured and needled the contents of virtually everything we take into our bodies. And we have done it for the same two reasons; the whim of a tinkerer or the profit-hunger of an uncaring corporation executive."

Hot War on the Consumer, edited by David Sanford (Pitman, 1969), is a collection of articles from *The New Republic.* Even after six years the articles by Sanford, Nader, Ridgeway, Coles, and others are hardly dated. All 124 pages of part I are about the food and drug industry; there is an excellent section on the pricing and advertising of drugs. The emphasis in this book is on the industry rather than the specific drugs involved.

Licit & Illicit Drugs by Edward M. Brecher and the editors of *Consumer Reports* (Little, Brown, paperback, 1973) is highly recommended as a fair and well-written look at drugs that does not neglect the problems posed by our legal drugs. Brecher has some very practical suggestions about drug control and recognizes that passing laws about a substance's legality or illegality is hardly a solution to the substance's abuse potential. The book also has a fine historical perspective on drugs, showing that drug problems are hardly new on the American scene.

Nutrition Scoreboard: Your Guide to Better Eating by Michael Jacobson (from Center for Science in the Public Interest, 1779 Church Street, N.W., Washington, DC 20036) has its own formula for determining food values. Foods are "scored" for nutritional value by brand name. Many practical tips for supermarket survival are presented. An excellent reference and resource book.

Supermarket Counter Power by Adeline Garner Shell (Warner Paperback Library) is subtitled "The Intelligent Food Shopper's Guide to Eating Better for Less Money." The book is aimed at homemakers and even includes recipes. The book is a nice combination of home economics, consumerism, and nutrition education.

The Supermarket Handbook: Access to Whole Foods by Nikki and David Goldbeck (Harper & Row) is a new release that I have not yet read. The book is described by the publisher as a guide to shopping the supermarket like a health food store with a brand-by-brand guide to getting the best nutrition for every food dollar. Sounds good.

200,000,000 Guinea Pigs by John G. Fuller (G. P. Putnam's, 320 pages) is less fanatic but even more frightening than *Consumer Beware*. Fuller is more a scientist than Hunter and includes in his study cosmetics and the ethical drug industry as well as the food technologists.

Multi-Media Resources

The Persuasion Box is a multi-media learning tool created by Jeffrey Schrank to explore the language of manipulation. It is designed for use in an English class for a two-day or longer unit or for individualized learning in a resource center. The box contains: (1) *From Symbols to Psycho-Sell* — a 43-frame filmstrip examining the persuasion techniques of advertising. Topics include "Symbols," "Ads and Personality Holes," "Love and Sex as Persuasion," and "Techniques of Psycho-Sell." Each of the 43 ads is analyzed in detail. Because the filmstrip is an in-depth examination of visual images, the usual recorded narration is replaced by a 10,000-word teaching guide. Discussion, based on the images shown, takes place during the filmstrip. It will take at least one class period to use. (2) *The Propaganda Game* — a learning game for two or more players that serves as a primer in the methods of language manipulation. (3) *I Can Sell You Anything* — Wrighter's 225-page paperback explaining the most commonly used weasels, fads, legalisms and tricks of persuasion via mass media. The book is supplied as a teacher's reference but it can also be used for individual assignments. (4) *The Claim Game* — gives students a chance to match wits with professional persuaders. The Claim Game both teaches and tests acquired knowledge, for one student or an entire class (5) *The Art of Honest Deception* — a spirit master (good for 150-plus copies) explaining the nine most commonly used linguistic tricks of the trade in advertising claims. (6) One or more 16mm TV commercials — for group discussion or as a collector's item. (7) *Idea Guide* — a sort of "teacher's manual" to give more ideas and suggestions for the persuasion unit. *The Persuasion Box* is available for $38.50 from The Learning Seed Company, 145 Brentwood, Palatine, IL 60067.

Advertising: The Image Makers is a multi-media kit consisting of a single sound filmstrip, a poster of imitation ads, thirty student booklets and six magazine ads referred to in the filmstrip. The filmstrip tells how one advertising agency tried to sell Sunkist lemons to teenage girls as a hair rinse and bath additive — it worked. The strip is well produced and entertaining but gives only basic information about the making of ads. The student workbook contains a series of suggestions for do-it-yourself ads to illustrate slogans, brand names, selling copy, emotional appeals, and a TV story-board.

The kit is nicely done and could serve as an introduction to junior high students. Older students deserve a little more depth and at least a glance at the darker side of the advertising world. In order to gain the cooperation of an ad agency the creators of the kit stayed away from any criticism of commercials. The narrator even points out as fact the industry's claim that without advertising products would cost more.

Reasonably priced at $39.95 from Xerox Educational Publications, Education Center, Columbus, OH 43216.

The Food and Drug Administration: A Nation's Watchdog (two-part filmstrip from Guidance Associates, Pleasantville, NY 10570) is an excellent filmstrip that does not bore students in spite of what might seem an unexciting topic. The presentation is critical of the FDA's relation to business, but does present a balanced picture.

Ann's Additive Story: Its Meaning to Your Food and Health (35-frame filmstrip with reading script for $5.50 from Manufacturing Chemists Association, 1825 Connecticut Avenue, N.W., Washington, DC 20009) is not a very good filmstrip, but it does present the industry's side of the story on food additives. It assures the viewer that food additives are safe and that the manufacturers are concerned about the safety of the eating public.

Advertising and the Consumer (one-part 16-minute filmstrip with a 30-minute recorded interview from Current Affairs, 24 Danbury Road, Wilton, CT 06897) shows how media are used to influence the consumer decision, especially through emotional hooks. The interview concerns the need for regulation to stop deceptive advertising.

Films

A Chemical Feast is made from two segments of the old TV series, *The Great American Dream Machine.* Comedian Marshall Efron plays a TV cook in the first segment showing viewers how to make a modern lemon cream pie — "factory fresh, factory approved. No lemons, no eggs, no cream, just pie." In the second segment, Efron invites viewers to play the creative playfoods game. Creative playfoods are those miracles of food technology created for fun and profit — your fun and the creator's profits. His examples include Froot Loops (spelled froot because they contain no fruit), dehydrated french fries, Kool-Aid, and a chemical topping.

Efron's satirical skits on the absurdities of marketing and consumerland are certainly the most entertaining bits of solid consumer education ever committed to film (11 minutes, color, sale $165, rental $20 from Benchmark Films, 145 Scarborough Road, Briarcliff Manor, NY 10510; rental also from Viewfinders, Box 1665, Evanston, IL 60204.

Brand Names and Labeling Games contains two more Marshall Efron segments. In "Brand Names" he points out that the very same product (bleach, MSG, aspirin) can vary widely in price, according to brand name. His general conclusion is that "Brand X" is a better buy than the well-known brands. The second segment is the least valuable of the four on these two films. In "Labeling Games" he points out the confusing way in which olives are graded for size (9 minutes, color, rental $20, sale $145, also from Benchmark films).

Food: Green Grow the Profits is THE film to use in a unit on food. It is a strong investigative documentary from ABC-TV.

This hard-hitting film examines where America's food comes from today and why it tastes the way it does. The premise of the film is that control of the growing, processing, and marketing of many foods in the United States has become big business —*agri*business. While supporters of agribusiness claim that this concentration results in efficiency and quality, the film reveals that the entrance of industrial giants into the food business has not always coincided with sound nutrition, good taste, or consumer economy.

The major aspects of agribusiness are examined — machines replace or help workers, penned animals are fed chemically enriched feed that will make them grow bigger faster, tough tomatoes are bred for better shipping qualities, and fertilizers and preservatives are used heavily and beyond safety regulations. Highly recommended (56 minutes, color, sale $600, rental $55, from Macmillan Films, 34 MacQuesten Pkwy, South, Mount Vernon, NY 10550).

Buy, Buy presents both the Jekyll and Hyde of the advertising world.

It features interviews with directors of television commercials and shows bits of the filming of a cosmetic ad and one for Philips Milk of Magnesia which takes place in Laxativeland.

The central fact of advertising, according to one director, is: "We're professional and the consumer is an amateur. The best commercials are the ones you walk away from but they later come back to you."

Buy, Buy gives three specific examples of advertising techniques, something the other two films avoid. A director notes that wide-angle lenses make "images explode . . . so a Capri can look like a Ferrari." In the Philips commercial the announcer is told to wear glasses to give him more authority. Another director explains that those ads which show tires running over glass and nails and sharp objects are a simple matter of editing – the parts where the tires failed are omitted, thus giving the impression of tire invulnerability.

Buy, Buy is the only film in this list that voices the often-heard view of ad people that commercials are severely limited in their power to persuade. One director admits, "They can make people more aware and that's about it."

Buy, Buy raises many questions for discussion. It also delves into the values of ads and their makers. Some of the interviews are weak and repetitive, but *Buy, Buy* still ranks as the most honest film available about television commercials (directed by Donald MacDonald, who also did *The Season*; sale $250, rental: inquire, from Churchill Films, 662 North Robertson Boulevard, Los Angeles, CA 90069).

60 Second Spot: The Making of a Television Commercial is not so much about the making of a commercial as it is about the making of a short film. *60 Second Spot* hardly acknowledges the existence of the ad agency and instead concentrates on the problems of casting, selecting a location, and shooting with the right light and atmosphere. This film, technically the best of the three shorts on commercials, is the one that says least about advertising. *60 Second Spot* could just as well be about the making of a scene from a feature film.

The film's subject matter is a 7-Up ad in which a British military commander and his aide trek through Middle Eastern sand dunes to escort a caravan of 7-Up trucks. Their campy conversation makes it clear that British imperialism exists to make the world safe for 7-Up. Although intended as satiric, the commercial contains enough truth to be ironic. One wonders what its effect would be if the actors had an American accent, or if one were a Kissinger-type.

60 Second Spot, like *Stalking the Wild Cranberry*, the next film on this list, emphasizes the great pains taken for the best possible footage and presents the filmmakers as dedicated professionals. One of its most fascinating sequences shows dozens of actors reading the same lines trying out for the roles of the two male actors. As in *Stalking*, the finished commercial is shown at the end of the film.

In the final evaluation, *60 Second Spot* must be classified as an entertaining and classy film about filmmaking rather than a behind-the-scenes look at the world of advertising. Nice but innocuous (25 minutes, color, sale $325, rental inquire from Pyramid Films, Box 1048, Santa Monica CA 90406).

Stalking the Wild Cranberry: The Making of a TV Commercial is sponsored by the American Association of Advertising Agencies. As a sponsored film, *Stalking* is itself an ad for the "dedicated professionals" who make television commercials. It provides as much behind-the-scenes nitty gritty as the oil company ads showing oilmen as beleaguered conservationists on the side of the little guy and the American Way. In spite of its limitations, the film is useful in classes studying television or advertising.

Stalking the Wild Cranberry presents a condensed version of the making of a Post Grape-Nuts commercial in which Euell Gibbons claims he sprinkles wild cranberries on his morning bowl of Grape-Nuts. The process of making a storyboard and deciding on the multitude of details before actual shooting is shown in a series of "re-enacted" conversations among Benton & Bowles agency people. The discussions are so condensed they appear quite staged and unreal. Using actors who sound like real people would have been better than using real people who sound like actors. Nothing is said about money — Gibbons is not "hired," he is simply "available."

The people who make the commercial are shown as men and women who take great care and make Herculean efforts to obtain the best possible work. They are also "human" people who can sit around at night after a hard day's filming in the Colorado mountains and joke and play the piano. That ad people are "good guys" seems to be the prime propaganda message of the film.

The film does give a few limited insights into the making of a television commercial — great effort is taken to obtain the best film, many people are involved, and sixty feet of film are thrown away for every foot used.

A topic students often discuss after viewing the film is that of endorsements and credibility. Why would a man like Gibbons, supposedly dedicated to natural foods, agree to promote a product of General Foods, an archenemy of the organic food people? I wonder whether Gibbons knows that a vice-president for corporate research at General Foods said, "We are moving gradually into a world of designed consumer foods. Natural farm produce such as milk, potatoes and grains are no longer just complete foods to be eaten as part of a meal. They have become ever-expanding sources of raw materials to be utilized as building blocks for new and more diverse synthetic foods."

Does the payment of huge fees for endorsements render all endorsements suspect? Can a television commercial be believed?

Even though *Stalking* is little more than a disguised commercial, it does raise interesting questions and will hold student interest. Recommended with reservations (14 minutes, sale $190, rental: inquire, from ACI Films, 35 West 45th Street, New York, NY 10036).

BLT is a film designed to combat a malady that afflicts most 1970's Americans — Eater's Alienation. People suffering from EA have come to believe food comes from a grocery store and only a few chemists know what is in all those packages so neatly arranged in supermarket rows and bathed in Muzak and fluorescent light all day. EA parents have only minor problems telling their children where babies come from, but few have mustered the courage to tell about eating cow meat and pigs. Just try to tell some four-year-old he or she is going to have cow meat for supper.

BLT begins with some rather romantic footage of pigs in early morning sunlight— all of which proves that almost anything looks nice in dawn's ethereal haze. The infamous mud bath is presented not as something dirty or ugly but as a sensuous experience — as all children secretly know. *BLT* filmmaker Art Ciocco may have vegetarian leanings. At least he believes the pigs have received bad press and is out to change their image. But these beautiful creatures, these cuddly and sensuous innocents, must serve man — so it's off to the slaughterhouse. A few converts to vegetarianism might be won; after all, vegetables don't scream so loud. But the doors remain mercifully shut and the viewer is asked to use his imagination. For a final shot the film moves to a restaurant where a patron calmly orders a bacon, lettuce, and tomato sandwich.

BLT is a nice film for children and also a philosophical reminder that we are other creatures rearranged and that life goes on only through the mutual slaughter and ingestion of various species (14 minutes, color, sale $190, rental: inquire, from ACI films, 35 West 45th Street, New York, NY 10036; Oh, the music in *BLT* is provided by Michael Bacon).

Harold and Cynthia explores the impact of advertising on people. Harold and Cynthia are two ordinary people who meet at a bus stop and are attracted to each other. But their attempts to establish a relationship are distorted by Madison Avenue messages that tell them importance and value are measured by the corporate products you use and media ideals to which you conform.

The simple animation changes to live action to present actual commercials that Harold and Cynthia see: "Smoke this and win the girl of your dreams," "Spray on a little of this and he'll follow you anywhere."

Harold and Cynthia have difficulty getting in touch with themselves or each other. The simple animation style conveys perfectly the emptiness of their world. Only when they go to a place of no advertising does the animation style become fuller and they are able to dance, to express joy and tenderness, Many viewers will consider the ending a bit overdone — advertising is a factor contributing to alienation but is hardly the sole cause.

The sound track uses "appropriate" pop tunes unobtrusively — "Sounds of Silence" is done with a solo flute. The film is bound to have some appeal for almost any audience and makes its point clearly and with visual interest (10 minutes, color, animation, rental $15, sale $150, from The Eccentric Circle, P.O. Box 155, Washington Depot, CT. 06794).

2

Nonverbal Communication:

Detecting Deception

in Communication

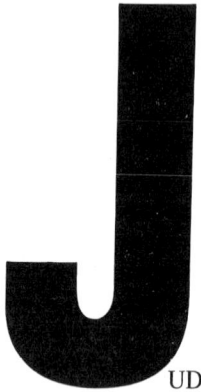

JUDGING FROM paperback book covers there is a sexy new "science," popularly known as body language, that enables anyone who knows a few tricks of the trade to immediately read the minds and feelings of near strangers. All one needs to know, the book covers imply, is the hidden meaning of an assortment of body gestures. The select few who have learned the key to these hidden meanings can determine if another person agrees or not, no matter what words are used, or if a companion of the opposite sex is ready to jump into bed or practice newly learned karate skills.

The popularization of the fledgling science of kinesics and proxemics paints a picture of an art that is half astrology and half party game. This is unfortunate since these relatively recent studies help the student of communication to study the concealed part of the iceberg. Schools have dealt largely with iceberg tips such as speaking and writing at the expense of that ninety percent of communication that is nonverbal.

Instead of teaching nonverbal communication as the next best thing to palmistry (or ignoring it as just a fad sparked by a few best-selling books) it can be studied as a means of increasing communication awareness. Everyone already has a solid grasp of sending and receiving nonverbal messages, but this understanding is largely unconscious. To increase this level of awareness is to help increase the ability to communicate, detect deception, and reduce ambiguity.

The ideas and teaching suggestions presented here are designed to develop awareness of some nonverbal, environmental aspects of communication. It is this refinement of awareness that is the most important objective of this chapter rather than the learning of any particular "secret meanings." All communication has present in it some degree of deception, whether intentional or not. By learning to observe nonverbal clues some of that deception can be detected.

We will consider three kinds of "listening between the lines" here. Kinesics or the language of gestures; proxemics or the language of personal space; and the messages exchanged between humans and the immediate environment.

KINESICS — THE LANGUAGE OF GESTURE

Two humans alone in a room carrying on a rather ordinary conversation exchange an overwhelming 200 to 5000 bits of information per second. Only a tiny percentage of this avalanche of informational exchange is verbal. The majority that remains is concerned with body movements and position.

Anthropologist Raymond Birdwhistell — as much the father of kinesics as anyone — began studying body movement to see if gestures such as scowls, laughs, and other commonly accepted signals were assigned the same meanings the world over. He found that "as far as we know, there is no single facial expression, stance, or body position which conveys the same meaning in all societies." As Birdwhistell studied body movement in more detail, using slow-motion films, he found an analogy between spoken language and body movement language. Just as speech can be broken down into sounds, words, sentences, and paragraphs, body movements could also be subdivided into units of meaning. He called the smallest observable motion a kine and a significant movement a kineme, thus paralleling the linguistic morph and morpheme.

Although students of body language estimate that over 700,000 distinct gestures can be produced by a combination of facial expressions, postures, movements of arms, hands and fingers, each culture accepts only a handful as meaningful. Birdwhistell estimates there are only about fifty or sixty kinemes that Americans use for the face and head.

To become even a fourth-rate kinesic scientist requires hundreds of hours of practice, especially with slow-motion films of human interaction. No one or two books or even a day or week of careful people-watching will produce an expert in body language. But an explanation of a few of the more obvious body language messages and some practice in their detection will help raise the communication-awareness level of students. We will consider only a few movements here concerning gestures, postures, eyes, and facial expressions. These meaningful gestures were selected not because they are the most revealing or the most commonly agreed upon among students of kinesics, but because they are relatively easy to observe and even interpret.

A distinction should be made here between gestures and signals. Signals are body movements made with the conscious intent to communicate — thumbing a ride, raising a hand to seek recognition in a group, a handshake. Gestures are movements made without a conscious intent to communicate; in fact, gestures are often made without the awareness of the person gesturing. They are often habits that have become part of the person's nonverbal vocabulary just as certain stock phrases and clichés have become part of his or her verbal vocabulary. Some of the most common gestures are described below.

One very common gesture, the hand-to-chin movement, sometimes with one finger pointed upward, frequently communicates a period of evaluation. An easily recognized example of this gesture is Rodin's famous sculpture of "The Thinker." The hand-to-chin gesture lends itself easily to interpretation, yet should never be assigned a meaning like a word. D-o-g has a limited number of meanings no matter which sentence it is used in, but a gesture cannot be interpreted out of context of the nonverbal equivalent of a sentence. There can never be a dictionary of body language gestures. Kinesic researchers are more concerned with taking inventory than in speculating about possible meanings of gestures. The hand-to-chin movement is only one of many gestures that are frequently used to signal "I'm evaluating that proposal or question." Sitting back in a chair with hands clasped behind the head, looking away from the person asking for a decision and handling an object on the desk, or even gazing at a point somewhere near the ceiling often gives the same evaluation signal.

If we were to search for one gesture that comes the closest to being able to have a single meaning, it might be the nose-rub *while expressing an opinion*. This gesture most often expresses doubt or rejection. If you ask someone, "Did you like the movie?" and the person replies, "Yes," while rubbing his nose, he probably means, "No" or at least, "It was only fair." When verbal and gestural messages conflict, chances are that the nonverbal message is the more accurate. We have learned to verbally protect what we want to conceal, but very few people can bring their gestures into congruence with the untruth. A few body language experts have used this fact with remarkable results in examining prospective jurors to determine their true bias.

Finger-wagging is often used by people in authority toward their underlings. It resembles a hitting motion and can be considered an abbreviated acting out of the impulse to hit something. For this reason the gesture is often perceived by the recipient as a threat even though the sender of the message would vehemently deny that any threat was implied. Sometimes a speaker will use eyeglasses or a pointer as an extension of the hand. In either case the gesture does emphasize the point being made, but also tends to make the audience a bit more hostile.

The gesture of covering one's face with one or both hands is close to universal although its meaning varies considerably with the circumstance. According to Henry Calero and Gerald Nierenberg, police who are experts in questioning criminal suspects report that a person talking with a hand over mouth is almost always either lying or, at least, unsure. Even Charles Darwin observed that the hand-to-mouth gesture is used throughout the world but he considered it an expression of astonishment. The gesture is sometimes used in imitation of the ostrich and nonverbally expresses the feeling "I don't want to know what is happening." Since the face is the most obvious symbol or locus of the self, hiding the face expresses a desire to hide oneself. Children will often perform some kind of hiding gesture when they feel guilty or are being scolded.

By observing children, researchers were first able to define the "defensive beating posture." One child about to strike another, usually in the course of play, will often hold his or her palm facing out with fingers curled over into a crude sort of fist. The hand will be in front of the head. If the child makes the same gesture, but holds the hand back more toward the side of the head, researchers have observed he or she is unlikely actually to land a blow. Such a gesture is a defensive warning, therefore called the defensive beating gesture. Adults rarely use this gesture but its remnants can be seen in a gesture in which the palm is placed on the back of the neck.

Often this defensive gesture is disguised as a grooming movement. A driver who pulls in too quickly in front of another car often does a quick "grooming" movement through the hair, followed by a hand-to-neck gesture.

Many grooming gestures have to be classified as some kind of body language rather than as utilitarian movements to improve appearance. Women with long hair can often be observed grooming their hair to the point of distraction. A flurry of grooming gestures often accompanies nervousness associated with being seen in public by a large number of people.

The formation of a steeple configuration with the fingertips is a gesture most often associated with a person speaking from a position of confidence. Watch out for the opponent in poker who steeples while bidding. Unless, of course, he's a very good poker player and knows all about how to bluff even in body language.

These hand gestures constitute a barely adequate introduction to the realm of body language. In addition to gestures another area of study in the confines of kinesics is posture.

A group of people sitting around a table arguing the pros and cons of a proposal will often indicate their state of mind by their posture. Researchers have found that we often indicate agreement with what another person is saying by mirroring that person's posture. In other words, congruent attitudes are often revealed by congruent postures. In a group of six people sitting around a table three are sitting at about a 45-degree angle from the table with their legs crossed. The other three are leaning over the table parallel to its edge. A fair guess would be that the three with the same posture have the same "stance" on whatever is being discussed.

A person with arms crossed at the chest and seated with legs crossed might be using this closed posture as a defense, similar to the gathering-in a baby does as if to regain the fetal shape from the womb. But such a posture could also mean the person is cold or uncomfortable. Postures, like gestures, can be accurately interpreted only in the context of the situation.

A person seated and listening to a proposal which would involve taking action often indicates a response by posture. A person who sits back in the chair (perhaps with hands clasped behind the head) is putting the proposal at a distance. On the other hand, the person who leans forward, who sits on the edge of the chair, is tending toward involvement. Of course, body language interpretation cannot tell what the nature of that involvement might be.

A group standing together and talking, say at a party or on a playground, communicates by posture if newcomers are welcome or not. A tightly closed circle is a sign for others to stay away unless invited, while a more open formation lends itself to being joined by others.

Another aspect of kinesics that deserves study is eye behavior. We have an elaborate code of culturally sanctioned eye behavior, probably because the eye is most revealing in nonverbal terms. To look at another person is not only to take in that person's being but also to reveal a bit of oneself. The eye cannot take without also giving of the self. In the face of such self-revelation kinesic ritual arises.

Imagine two people, neither intimate friends nor total strangers, meeting in a hallway — John and Mary. When Mary talks, she tends to look away from John. She glances at him from time to time, usually as she pauses at the end of a phrase or sentence. When she does look at John, he responds in some way by nodding his head or saying "uh-huh" to indicate he is listening.

Mary then looks away again. Her glances at John last about as long as her glances away from him. When she comes to the end of what she wants to say, she will look at John for a longer time.

Now John speaks. Mary now spends most of her time looking at John, much more than when she was doing the talking. The next time John and Mary meet they will control their eyes in much the same manner, yet neither could give an accurate verbal or written explanation of the rules they follow in determining where to look.

This conversational eye traffic control does make sense. Looking away while talking allows the speaker to gather his or her thoughts. Looking back at the person spoken to signals some sort of feedback. The head-nodding is feedback or at least a show of politeness. Variations from this standard procedure are significant and indicate greater or lesser degrees of intimacy or interest.

We mentioned earlier that children will sometimes hide their faces while receiving a scolding. The same avoidance is achieved by simply avoiding eye contact, thereby saying "I'm not really here."

Two strangers passing on a sidewalk in a large city act much like two cars passing on the road at night and mutually dimming their lights. Each person can eye the other until about eight feet apart. At this point they cast their eyes down or away. But in so doing their behavior communicates both "I don't know you" and "I respect you enough not to stare."

Among middle-class whites this behavior is amazingly standard even though it is never formally taught. Part of the standard eye language behavior in America is that people don't stare at strangers. Any glance longer than three seconds is likely to produce an emotional reaction in a stranger. This is why two people cannot stand close together and stare at each other in the eye for more than a few seconds without breaking into defensive laughter.

American women who travel in Europe, the Middle East, and Latin America report they feel stared at on the streets. In France and Italy, for example, eye behavior rules permit men to stare intensely at women in public. They are not necessarily being fresh or making advances, they are simply speaking nonverbal Italian or French.

A person who violates the rules of eye contact behavior has a difficult time communicating. One who makes little eye contact with others gives the impression of not wanting to communicate or become involved. One early warning sign of possible autism in children is an infant's failure to look at his or her parents.

Some students of eye behavior have uncovered what might be a cause of communication problems between blacks and whites. They found that in poor black families, people look directly at one another less often than do people in white middle-class families. This could account for the often reported fact that blacks meeting whites sometimes feel stared at while whites report blacks avoid their eyes. Also, the pattern of looking at a person while listening and away while talking is often reversed when blacks talk to blacks. When whites and blacks converse, they are therefore likely to be speaking different body language "dialects" and using different eye behavior.

Edward Hess, a University of Chicago psychologist, has found that when a person is looking at something especially interesting the pupils of the eyes dilate — become larger. He found that when he slipped pictures of nudes into a stack of photographs he showed his male assistant, he was able to tell by the width of the pupil opening exactly when he was looking at the nudes. The change in pupil size is very minute, however, and usually instruments are required to read the change accurately, but it is possible that the ability to detect a change in pupil size is part of what is commonly called intuition or even, among card players, luck.

In addition to gestures, postures, and eye behavior, kinesics is interested in facial expressions.

Ray Birdwhistell has volunteered perhaps the most startling theory to come out of kinesics. He believes that physical appearance is often culturally programmed. In other words, we learn our looks — we are not born with them. A baby has generally unformed facial features. A blob here and a lump there have the potential of becoming almost any expression. A baby, according to Birdwhistell, learns where to set the eyebrows by looking at those around — family and friends. This helps explain why the people of some regions look so much alike. New Englanders or Southerners have certain common facial characteristics that cannot be explained by genetics. Scalp placement is not set at birth, it is learned after, as is the exact shape of the mouth. In fact, the final mouth shape is not formed until well after permanent teeth are set. For many, this can be well into adolescence.

A husband and wife together for a long time often come to look somewhat alike. We learn our looks from those around us. This is perhaps why even in the United States there are areas where people smile more than those in other areas. The South is the part of the country where the people smile most frequently. In New England they smile less, and in the western part of New York state still less. Many Southerners find cities such as New York cold and unfriendly, partly because people on Madison Avenue smile less than people on Peachtree Street in Atlanta. People in densely populated urban areas also tend to smile and greet each other in public less than do people in rural areas and small towns.

To study facial expressions takes great time and patience. A University of Pennsylvania team of evolutionary biologists spent five years studying how people used their tongues unconsciously. They found that children show their tongues when they are engaged in difficult tasks or involved in awkward social situations such as receiving a scolding. They then found that adults use their tongues in a similar way. Adults too show their tongues during tasks requiring intense concentration and in socially threatening situations. They further found that gorillas and orangutans speak essentially the same tongue language as humans — but the animals show their tongues more often.

Possible Discussion Questions for Kinesics

1. Compile a list of signals (handshake, wave, etc.) and a list of gestures (folding arms, steepling, crossing legs, etc.).

2. As a sort of awareness test of body language ask students if they know the difference between how women and men move their arms when they walk. Have some males and females walk in front of the class and base further discussion on the observation of arm swing differences. Have males try the female arm movement and vice versa and comment on how the role-reversal feels. The answer to "why" the arm swings are different is beyond the realm of a class discussion, but is at least a good topic for speculation.

3. Have two volunteers (or the entire class in pairs) stare at one another and attempt to maintain a straight face. Maybe the class could even select the "straight face champ." Discuss feelings and speculate why people respond to a stare with a blush or giggle.

4. Have students who are members of minority or ethnic groups or who have traveled or lived in other countries report on nonverbal differences among those groups.

5. Bring a television set to class. Find a quiz or talk show or some program involving non-actors. Examine the body movements in terms of communication. Watch for conversational traffic signals, eye behavior, grooming gestures, hand movements, and postures.

6. If the school has a videotape unit, try taping the body language of volunteers. This might best be done in connection with the following suggestion.

7. Have three to five students stand (or sit so they can be seen by the rest of the class) in front of the class and talk about whatever they want for five to ten mintues. The rest of the class serves as observers, each watching for kinesic meaning in only one specialized area — head move-

ments, eye contact, hand gestures, posture, facial expressions. After the discussion the observers comment on the body language patterns of the group holding the discussion. Do this with a number of groups so that all or most students take part as both observers and the observed. Videotape each discussion for confirmation of various observations.

Activities Requiring Work Outside the Classroom

1. Assign individuals or small groups of students the job of becoming specialists in one specific body language gesture. Assigned areas of specialization could include eye contact in conversation, staring, pedestrian traffic on a crowded street or hallway, leg crossing, signals used to break off a conversation, greetings, saying goodbye, posture when seated, touching others, hand-to-mouth movements, tongue movement outside of mouth, hiding the face, defensive beating posture, grooming movements, gestures (not signals) used often in sports, hands in pockets, different kinds of walks, smiles, the gestures of children, etc.

Have each student become a people-watcher, cataloging how people use a particular gesture or movement. Report to the whole class on the observations. To assign students to watching for nonverbal behavior in general is far less effective than assigning one or two specific gestures or situations.

2. Some students might try experiments involving breaking some commonly accepted rule of nonverbal behavior and reporting on the responses they evoke. Their unconventional behavior might be staring at people in public places, having a conversation in which they rarely look at the other person (or in which they regard the other person with extreme eye contact intensity), sitting in an elevator or standing in a nearly empty bus, walking against the flow of traffic in a crowded hall or sidewalk, standing too far away or too close to someone in a conversation, or using exaggerated hand movements in conversation.

3. Students with photographic equipment could prepare a super-8 film or slide presentation showing some of the nonverbal messages they observed while doing activity number one.

4. Have a group of students make a candid film of public behavior — people in a bus station or airport, a crowded hallway or street, a line, a cafeteria, or any public area. Examine the nonverbal behavior.

5. Someone with an infant at home could experiment to see if the baby does indeed react to a piece of paper with two eye-sized black dots in a way similar to the way the baby responds to a human face.

PROXEMICS — THE LANGUAGE OF SPACE

Kinesics is the study of bodily movements while proxemics involves learning how the body utilizes space in the immediate environment.

Each person carries an invisible bubble of personal space which extends from the skin out to about eighteen inches. We are not normally aware of the personal space bubble until others attempt to "invade" that space without permission. An excellent way to demonstrate the existence of this invisible shield is to conduct man-in-the-street interviews.

The interviewer should look like a typical in-the-street survey-gatherer, complete with clipboard and a series of questions about some product or local issue. The questions the interviewer asks are unimportant, what is really under study is the reaction of the person being interviewed when his or her personal space is violated.

The interviewer begins about two feet away and gradually moves closer to the person being questioned. As the interviewer moves past the eighteen-inch shield, the person under question will very likely move back. If the interviewer again moves into the newly established area of personal privacy, the other person will again move back. If this is repeated, the resulting action will resemble a proxemic ballet, characterized by repeated "attacks" and "retreats."

Not all persons stopped will retreat, some will begin to retreat but will quickly assume a stance that says, "Here is where I stand my ground." A most common stance for that body language message is arms folded across the chest and the body turned at a 45-degree angle to the interviewer.

The moral of this little experiment (which can be seen in the film *Invisible Walls* described on page 59) is that we don't let people into our personal space unless they have some business there. We even define friends in proxemic terms — a "close" friend is someone we allow closer than others. Extreme closeness is allowed among deep friends, lovers, and professionals such as dentists and nurses who have a utilitarian reason for working within the personal space bubble.

The description of the invisible bubble of personal space as existing about eighteen inches from the skin is a purely American definition. Most other cultures place their shield closer to the body. If we talk to a person from the Middle East, Latin America, Italy, Spain, or Russia, we might find the experience uncomfortable. In ordinary conversation these peoples tend to stand closer together than do Americans.

Even within a society there are differences in proxemic language. American blacks use slightly different space language than whites. Studies have shown that whites prefer casual conversation at about 26-28 inches apart while blacks prefer a closer 21-24 inches. This difference might cause a black to consider whites distant while the white will consider blacks "pushy," thus influencing all verbal communication between them.

The distance we choose to stand from others is in itself a proxemic message. In general we stand closer to those we like than those we don't. Friends stand closer together than mere acquaintances and acquaintances closer than strangers. There is some evidence to suggest that pairs of women stand closer when talking than do pairs of men, but no one knows why this might be true. Other experiments have shown that in intimate situations introverts keep slightly greater distances apart than do extroverts. Most people unconsciously stand farther from people with physical handicaps, thus adding to the feeling of isolation these people often report.

Animals have a kind of personal space mechanism called "flight distance." The flight distance is that distance from the skin an animal will allow a potential enemy to approach before taking flight. A lion tamer uses flight distances to coax a lion to back up. What appears to the audience as training (or as a courageous trainer and a cowering lion) is really no different from the action we observed between the interviewer and the person on the street. As a general rule the larger the animal, the greater the distance it keeps between itself and its enemies. An antelope will flee when the intruder is as much as five hundred yards away.

This concept of personal space can be extended to include the sense of territoriality and helps explain other human phenomena. To extend personal space in this way is to leave the realm of proxemic science and enter that of speculation.

We can consider personal space as an extension of the self, the establishment of psychological rather than physical boundaries for where the self begins in space. This area of personal space is not really one bubble but a series of concentric circles. Some of the circles govern spacing in public, others with friends, others in formal and informal situations. Patriotism can be considered one of the farthest circles of someone who has internalized his nation's physical boundaries. To invade the nation, or even to launch verbal criticism, is to attack the person, to invade his space without permission.

Although only some people consider the nation as part of the extended self, everyone has some desire to stake out and mark or claim space as private, personal, his own. In fact, most school history courses are little more than an accounting of various attempts of people to claim territory as their own, thus giving rise to today's division of the world into nations.

Not only do we permanently and rather violently stake out claims to huge areas of land as a people, we also subtly and temporarily claim territories in public spaces. Public space is that area of space open to public access where no one can say, "I own this land" (a sidewalk, elevator, library) yet where the space must be temporarily used in such a way as to resemble ownership.

One unwritten but widely accepted rule of using public spaces is that when a lot of usable space is available, one should keep one's distance. A simple experiment again illustrates this rule. A student of proxemics went to a college library study hall and picked out a "victim" surrounded by empty chairs and sat down in the next seat. The "victims" in his experiment usually reacted with defensive gestures and uneasy shifts of posture or they edged away. When the experimenter not only sat down in the next chair but then proceeded to move it closer, the victim often fled. Rarely did the subjects protest verbally. For although people have strong feelings about the violation of personal space, they rarely talk about them.

Entering an elevator gives another example of the temporary claiming of public space and an elaborate but unwritten set of rules more detailed than any Amy Vanderbilt ever proposed. The first person in an empty

Nonverbal Communication

elevator is most likely to claim a corner by the controls or in the rear. The second person entering is most likely to stand in a corner across from the one occupied. The third and fourth passengers take up the remaining corners. A fifth will take the middle of the rear wall while the sixth is left with the center of the car. This is a basic pattern, but one that finds many exceptions. A group that enters together will tend to stand in a grouped fashion, signaling their existence as a unit.

In public spaces when we want to claim an area such as a table or bench for ourselves, we leave what proxemicists call territorial "markers." A bus passenger who wishes to have the seat next to him or her left unoccupied might hang a coat or place a package on the seat as a marker signaling to others, "I want this seat left empty." The marker usually works unless all other seats are taken.

Animals use similar devices. A bear will claw the bark from tree trunks to mark home territory and a deer secretes a smelly substance from a gland near the nostril. A wolf may urinate near the periphery of its territory and neighborhood dogs also mark space this way.

In addition to claiming public bench or table space people will claim a specific position at a table as an unconscious expression of their intentions. If a group is in the process of forming – say a jury yet to select its foreman – one of the people seated at either end of the table is most likely to be chosen foreman. And the person most likely to select such a seat is someone with social status and leadership ambitions. If only two people are to be seated at a table, they will most likely sit according to their preconceptions of what will happen. If they expect to compete, they will sit opposite each other. If they expect to cooperate at a task, they will sit next to each other and if they expect ordinary conversation, they are likely to sit at right angles.

Robert Sommer, a researcher in proxemics, found that seating arrangements at a table influence the amount of conversation that takes place.

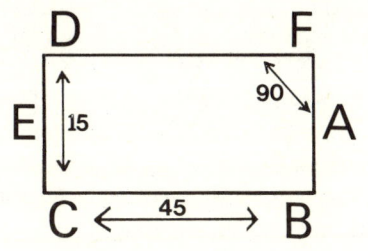

He made random observations at a rectangular table in an institutional cafeteria. He found the most common path of conversation was between persons at positions F and A, where 90 conversations were noted. Half as many, 45, were observed between people at positions C and B and only 15 between people seated across from each other at C and D.

Questions and Experiments for Further Study of Proxemics

1. The following experiment/game is adapted from Mark L. Knapp's instructor's guide to the text *Nonverbal Communication in Human Interaction.* It is best conducted before the class is even aware that nonverbal communication is the subject under study.

Divide the class into standing groups of three and give each person one card with instructions. The cards should have a large A, B or C on the back to identify group members. Tell the class only that one person in each group is an observer but give no other idea about what is being observed.

> *Instruction to person A:* You are going to carry on a five minute conversation with person C. Try to agree with C on a topic to talk about. VERY slowly (note VERY SLOWLY) you should begin to inch in closer towards person C during the discussion. Make your move appear natural. See how close you can get before C backs up or somehow reacts to your movement. If you can force C to back up, you win a genuine "people mover" award.
>
> *Instruction to person B:* You are the observer. Stand close enough to see A and C in detail, yet not so close as to be part of their conversational grouping. You are to watch the distance between A and C as well as their eye contact.
>
> *Instruction to person C:* You are to carry on a conversation with person A. Try to decide on some topic to talk about. Find some topic that A has strong opinions about and express your opinion as exactly opposite of A's. Make your disagreement appear as sincere as possible. As you begin to disagree, observe A's body movements — hand movements and body stance in particular.

Discussion of the exercise: discuss the reactions of person C to the forward movement of A. Ask both A and C for their feelings during the conversation. Have person B bring up any observation. Discuss eye contact. A videotape of the entire exercise could be helpful here.

2. Have some pairs of volunteers experiment with saying "You're

really wonderful" to each other while (a) across the room from each other, (b) twelve feet apart, (c) four feet apart, and (d) only one foot apart. Discuss the differences in feelings and the effect of the statement from the various distances. Try the same experiment but this time say, "Always put your trash in the waste basket."

3. Discuss the relationship between personal space, territoriality, and patriotism. DEBATE: Man's sense of territoriality is (a) Useful to the further development of the human race (b) Destructive to the further development of the human race.

4. Conduct some personal space invasion interviews as explained in this chapter. Record the results either in very detailed notes or with a hidden camera.

5. Have students experiment at various times during a week with their own conversational spacing. Try some conversations that are conducted at distances abnormally close and far. This is an example of a norm violation experiment — an excellent way to learn about nonverbal behaviors.

6. Assign students to finding or making pictures of signs of human territoriality — of people "marking" their territories and declaring boundaries. Exclude fences from this study since they are so obvious.

7. Devise and conduct an experiment with "markers." School libraries and cafeterias work well for such experiments.

8. Ride elevators as a form of field research on "space behavior in elevators" and report findings to the class.

9. Find an observation post from which to watch the temporary claiming of public space for personal use. Observers could stake out an observation post in a cafeteria, public or school bus, public benches, waiting areas, beaches, a nursery school, an airport, or any place where people have to line up and wait.

ENVIRONMENTAL COMMUNICATION

The study of body movements as communication and the study of personal space are new sciences, but they at least have names. The third area of the communication iceberg is as yet unnamed and has no well-known scholars or even popularizers. It is the communication or interchange that takes place between people and their immediate environment — a room, a machine, a city and its buildings. This constant interaction is a kind of nonverbal communication. Our environment shapes us in subtle and usually unnoticed ways.

The problem with environments is that their effects are often invisible to those inside. We don't know who discovered water, but it certainly wasn't a fish. Consider what it is like in a stuffy, airless room. People in such a room are often unaware that the room is stuffy until they walk outside or someone opens a window and they are reminded what fresh air feels like.

The experience of driving or flying into the downtown or industrial area of a city provides another example of the invisible nature of the immediate environment. From a distance the pall of pollution hanging over the area is easily seen. But once inside the environment of polluted air, it becomes normal and unnoticed.

If we are often unaware of the very quality of the air we breathe, there are likely to be many other facets of the immediate environment that we also do not notice. We do not read the communication from the environment and thereby lose some of our freedom to respond to it. The constant repetition of certain types of rooms, buildings, and cities influences the development of personality and indirectly communicates to the inhabitants, whether the inhabitants are aware that communication is taking place or not.

Another way to say this is to say that the colors, shapes, textures, and spaces in the environment in which people spend much time influence their feelings, moods, personality, likes and dislikes, behavior and identity. Take color for example.

Color, like air, is such a constant part of the environment that we tend to ignore its messages. Many people with perfect vision suffer from a sort of cultural color blindness. But even unnoticed color influences feelings. Experiments with both infants and adults show that blue light tends to lessen activity and produce a state of restfulness. The more tense a person is, the more blue will act as a tranquilizer.

Red, on the contrary, excites the nervous system, even to the point of irritation. If this page were to be printed on red paper, electrodes attached to your skin would show a definite increase in muscle tension, restlessness, blood pressure, and eye movements compared with your reaction to the white pages. Studies have found that patients in hospital rooms painted bright red for the sake of the experiment require more attention from nurses than patients in rooms painted in more subdued colors.

At the University of Kansas art museum, investigators tested the effects of different colored walls on two groups of visitors to an exhibit of paintings. For the first group the room was painted light beige; for the second, dark brown. Movement of each group was traced by an electrical system under the carpet. The experiment revealed that those who entered the dark brown room walked more quickly, covered more area, and spent less time in the room than the people in the beige environment. Dark brown stimulated more activity, but the activity was concluded sooner.

Not only the choice of colors but also the general appearance of a room communicates and influences those inside. One experiment presented subjects with photographs of faces that were to be rated in terms of energy and well-being. Three groups of subjects were used; each was shown the same photos, but each group was in a different kind of room. One group was in an "ugly" room that resembled a messy janitor's storeroom. Another group was in an average room — a nice office. The third group was in a tastefully designed living room with carpeting and drapes. Results showed that the subjects in the beautiful room tended to give higher ratings to the faces than did those in the ugly room. Other studies suggest that students do better on tests taken in comfortable, attractive rooms than in nondescript or ugly rooms.

Furniture arrangement within a room is a form of communication. Many American "living rooms" shout out "no one lives here, this is really a showroom." Others say very clearly that the television set is the center of attraction and make human conversation difficult.

An experiment in a doctor's office suggests that even a desk can influence patient feelings. With the desk separating doctor from patient, only ten percent of the patients were judged to be "at ease," but when the desk was removed, fifty-five percent of the patients were at ease in the office.

How classroom furniture is arranged also speaks about the values placed on the various kinds of interactions that could take place there. The traditional straight rows say that students' talking to each other is not an important part of the learning process. If that is true in a particular school, then that is a fitting arrangement. A circular arrangement accepts the fact that nonverbal messages are important and that students can learn from each other. A teacher who lectures to students seated in a circle but does not use student body language as feedback might just as well go back to the straight-row arrangement.

The rows-and-aisles arrangement tends to encourage teachers to notice students sitting in certain areas of the room more than others. As a general rule, those seated front and center participate in class discussions the most, while those at the edges and corners participate much less.

As a room influences those inside, so do the design and visual effect of the buildings in which the rooms are located. Buildings, even while only viewed from the outside, speak. They send messages that communicate conformity and dullness, coldness and isolation, or messages that help others feel warm and cheerful, comfortable, part of a group yet an individual.

How buildings influence behavior can be seen in the example of two New York public housing projects located across the street from each other. One is a typical high-rise, containing 150 families in 17 stories. The elevators, stairs, hallways and roof are freely roamed and ruled by criminals. The stories of what happens in the building are frightening.

Across the street is another project consisting of three six-story buildings in which two to three families share a hallway and six to twelve an entrance. The density of population in both projects is the same and construction costs were about the same. Yet this second project is nearly crime-free.

Urban planner Oscar Newman studied these two environments for three years, looking for clues to the spectacular difference in crime rates. He found that the crucial difference was the attitude of the tenants influenced by the building design. The crime-free, low-rise families were able to see what was happening in the mutually shared public spaces. A sense of territoriality developed that proved an effective defense against criminal activity. These people had no hesitation in calling the police when something suspicious was observed; they felt a responsibility for the shared space they could see.

In the crime-ridden high-rise the long impersonal corridors, lobbies, and stair shafts didn't "belong" to anyone, so no one felt responsibility for what took place in them. Since they belonged to no one, they could easily be taken over by criminal elements.

The design of school buildings has much to do with what feelings students have about learning and the school. Some schools are cold, hard places with even lighting that resemble factories. Others allow students to claim a space as their own and provide a variety of seating, lighting, textures, and color as part of the environment.

Defacing walls, whether by students in a school or employees in a new Manhattan office skyscraper, is often a reaction to a sterile building. Graffiti and wall-writing are a form of personalizing impersonal space, a way of placing on a bare surface the stamp of human activity. One approach to such "vandalism" is to offer "$100 reward for information leading to the arrest and conviction of anyone . . . . " Another is to provide places for inhabitants to show their presence (murals or graffiti walls) or to make surfaces so interesting they will not be defaced.

No building will change its inhabitants overnight, but those who must spend a large portion of the day or even of their life in a building can be shaped and changed by the messages of the building. One architect boasted he could design a house that could break up a marriage within a month. He could also probably design a school that would turn out a high rate of students who hate learning. Perhaps he could also do the opposite.

In designing the public spaces of buildings (and cities) architects and designers can make an area say, "This is a place for people to be together." Or they can design the environment to say, "This is a place where people are to be isolated. They will have to exert extra effort to be together here." Airport waiting areas with their rows of bolted chairs seem designed to minimize the possibility of contact. Often public spaces are intentionally designed to drive people away and into areas where they are more likely to spend money — bars, shops, and restaurants. Fast-food franchises with interior seating are carefully engineered to say, "You can stay here and eat, but don't stay too long — we need a fast turnover."

Much of the modern urban environment gives ambiguous messages. For the first time in history much of our environment must be labeled "artificial" or "imitation" something. It is increasingly difficult to find food, clothing, and housing materials that are not synthetic and designed to look like something else. An environment filled with plastics and chemical products posing as wood, metal, leather, cloth, and even living plants and grass must have some effect on those who live amidst the artificiality. The nonverbal message of such an environment is that things aren't always what they seem to be. Architect Kyoshi Izumi proposes that this imitation reality produces almost instinctive reactions. Subconsciously, he says, we resist the synthetic world and look for what is natural, organic, and "real."

His idea certainly receives support from the flood of advertising that attempts to sell the "organic," "natural," and "real." Of course, what is advertised as "natural" (or the "natural look") is created by factories and chemicals as often as not. The message of synthetic materials need not be low-quality goods or cheapness. Plastics have received a bad name and are often synonymous with what is cheap and unreal. In reality, plastic is an amazing invention, but its versatility has led manufacturers to use it only to imitate other things instead of developing plastic as a material in its own right.

In order to shape an environment that sends the messages we want, it is necessary to have designers and ordinary citizens aware of the environment as a system of nonverbal communication.

Questions and Experiments for Further Study of Environmental Communication

1. Administer an "Environmental Awareness" test, asking questions about the color of the floor outside the door, a description of the wall at the back of the room, and questions about things that are part of the students' everyday environment. Concentrate especially on colors. In one school the name of a locker manufacturing company was written on a metal tag on all two thousand school lockers, yet not one student could name the company. Discuss why everyday environments tend to become invisible.

2. Discuss student "hangouts," both in school and outside. How is space structured in such a way as to make these places useful and popular as hangouts? Discuss local neighborhoods and their nonverbal messages.

3. Discuss the school building in terms of its use of space. Are various arrangements used to separate upper- and underclass students? How does the school building either promote or discourage students from commu-

nicating with each other. Discuss the arrangement of space and furniture in the public areas — lounges, classrooms, library, cafeteria, offices, and lobbies. What does the main entrance to the school say to a visitor?

4. Find some aspect of the school environment that students see as sending negative nonverbal messages. Propose some ways to change this area.

5. Consider the school environment in terms of lighting, colors, and the nonverbal message of the building. What are the school colors? This question means the "real" colors, not the symbolic colors used for the athletic team. In other words, what colors predominate in the school building?

6. Invite the architect of the school or a member of the firm that built the school to talk to the class. Have questions ready based on your own observation of the nonverbal messages of the school.

7. Have each student select some building other than school or home that he or she enters fairly often. Write a report on that building in terms of what "message" it communicates by its colors, lighting, design, textures, furniture, space use, etc.

8. The physical reactions to different colors can be measured with a device such as a lie detector or a meter that measures galvanic skin response. The science department could probably make such a device for students to use to test reactions to color. A school version of a Galvanic Skin Response Meter sells for about $65 from BRS Foringer, 5451 Holland Drive, Beltsville, MD 20705; Edmund Scientific, Edscorp Building, Barrington, NJ 08007, has a less sensitive meter they call an "emotion meter" for under $20.

9. Have each student take a picture of some room in a house and write a report about the nonverbal message of that room. If no camera is available, use a picture from a magazine.

10. Take an environmental-awareness walk, noticing only color or buildings or textures or noise. Focus only on one or two nonverbal aspects of the environment. Write a report (or report verbally to the class) on the findings. This experiment could also be conducted during class time in the school building.

11. Why are certain walls vandalized and defaced while others escape such treatment? If the school has a graffiti problem, brainstorm a way to solve it that is not based on punishing those who write on walls.

RESOURCE GUIDE

Multi-Media Materials

Currently there is not a wide variety of films and filmstrips dealing with nonverbal communication. Acceptable material now available includes:

Body Language is a two-part sound filmstrip (total running time 20 minutes) which serves as a nice introduction to kinesics, but neglects proxemics and environmental communication. Stills of sculptures, paintings, commercials, magazine ads, and people waiting in airports are used to demonstrate various kinesic gestures. The strip also goes into a bit of theory by explaining the ideas of Harvard's Lawrence Frank who believes that body language originates in the tactile experience of infants.

Body Language is priced around $15 and certainly represents a good value for the money. From Multi-Media Productions, Box 5097, Stanford, CA 94305.

Nonverbal Communication is a box of twenty-five 11" x 14" heavy-duty cards and a 72-page teaching guide. Half the guide is a well-researched but dull overview of the study of nonverbal communication. The second part gives directions for 9 activities in a classroom using the 25 cards. One activity has a group of students go through a nonverbal version of the often-used "cooperative squares" exercise, while the rest of the class watches for nonverbal messages. Three other activities allow students to role-play various situations while others observe their nonverbal behavior. Five cards showing schematic diagrams of seating arrangements in a school and office can spark discussion of how such structured space influences communication. Five cards present large photos of people for students to diagnose meanings through facial expressions. The remaining cards showing room arrangements and a building design allow an exploration of the way rooms and buildings affect human interaction.

The kit is reasonably priced at $12.50 and does serve as an adequate introduction to the subject. From National Textbook Co., 8259 Niles Center Road, Skokie, IL 60067.

Exploring Nonverbal Communication is a two-part filmstrip; the first unit titled *Kinesics: Understanding Body Language,* communicates an amazing amount of information at rapid-fire speed. The photography is excellent and instructive, the narration well done, and the script clearly written and informative. Although intended for college underclassmen, the strip would work well as an introduction in a high school class.

Proxemics: Space in Human Perspective is a 12-minute look at how our use of space is a form of communication. As with *Kinesics,* this is professionally narrated and photographed. But it, in striking contrast, is filled with academic gobbledygook and vague generalities that make it hard to follow. The script is clogged with phrases such as "communicative responses dictated by sensory apparatus," "fixed and semi-fixed apparatus space" and "spatial and attitudinal orientation." In summary, the filmstrip on kinesics would be a welcome addition to any communication course, the one on proxemics less so. No written script is provided, but a few good teaching ideas are given in the brief guide.

Each filmstrip is $29.95 or both for $53.77 from Center for Advanced Study of Human Communication, 6186 Busch Blvd., Columbus, OH 43229.

Invisible Walls is a 16mm film about the walls eighteen inches from our bodies in which we Americans mentally encase ourselves. The film records how pedestrians were stopped for interviews only to have their "personal space" violated. Strangers who invade this eighteen inches of personal space are told in body language to back off or that their closeness is considered an attack. Such behavior is learned, the narrator points out, and is different from culture to culture. Americans are physically aloof compared to other cultures who also live in crowded cities. American children accept contact as a part of life, but soon learn to restrict touching to a highly limited set of conditions. The film concludes that with increases in city size and population we either have to learn to tolerate more invasions of our personal space or learn to enjoy physical closeness. Film is excellent for a discussion and a fine introduction to body language.

The 12-minute black-and-white film is available for a rental fee of about $10 from University of California, Extension Media Center, 2223 Fulton St., Berkeley, CA 94720; also from The Audio-Visual Education Center, University of Michigan, 416 Fourth St., Ann Arbor, MI 48103 for about $5.

A Reader's Guide to Books About Nonverbal Communication

Body Language by Julius Fast (Pocket Books) is the book that made "body language" part of the American vocabulary. The book still stands as one of the two easiest-to-read introductions to body language. *Body Language* is popular rather than scholarly, somewhat oversimplified but still well researched. The reading level is suitable for most high school or junior high students.

Inside Intuition: What We Know About Nonverbal Communication by Flora Davis (McGraw-Hill, hardcover, 1974) is more up-to-date than *Body Language,* even better researched, ranges further in the field of nonverbal communication, and is still written in a popular rather than scholarly style. Longer and more detailed than *Body Language, Inside Intuition* is the best introduction for all but those who find reading very difficult; the reading level is suitable for most high school students, but is a little more difficult than Fast's book. Also available in paperback.

The Hidden Dimension by Edward T. Hall (Doubleday Anchor paperback) is a basic work on nonverbal studies. Hall brings the mind of an anthropologist to communication and is particularly good when writing about differences between cultures and the use of public space. Hall's writing style is clear and simple. Both Davis and Fast rely rather heavily on Hall's original research. If you want information straight from the researcher instead of interpreted by someone else, this is the best book for a start. Hall's *The Silent Language* (Fawcett paperback) is less valuable as a starter and is concerned more with cultural differences.

How to Read a Person Like a Book by Gerard Nierenberg and Henry Calero (Pocket Books) is nicely illustrated, simply written, and ranks with Fast's book as the two simplest introductions. Very little attention is paid to public space and the environment; instead the book concentrates on kinesics, especially in business situations. To leaf through the 180-page paperback, looking only at the line drawings, is in itself an introduction to kinesics.

A World of Strangers by Lyn H. Lofland (Basic Books, 1973, hardcover) is a fascinating but little-known study of public space and behavior. Lofland surveys various devices used at different times in history to create social and psychological order in cities. She realizes that modern cities are shaped by the fact that strangers are now the rule rather than the exception. She is especially perceptive in observing public behavior (how old people colonize bus stations, for example), waiting styles, and our cultural privacy shield.

Personal Space: The Behavioral Basis of Design and *Tight Spaces: Hard Architecture and How to Humanize It* (Prentice-Hall paperbacks) by Robert Sommer are the two best books to consult on the use and abuse of public spaces. Sommer is a psychologist concerned about how buildings and public spaces influence behavior.

Tight Spaces, his most recent work, is well illustrated and written in a highly readable style. Its first chapter ranks among the best short, concise statements of the environment as a people-shaper.

Touching (Perennial Library) by Ashley Montagu is a massive 400-page paperback on the sense of touch and the value of physical contact in a society. Although few students will read the whole book, it is an excellent source to consult for the study of touch as communication.

Nonverbal Communication in Human Interaction (Holt, Rinehart and Winston, College Department) by Mark L. Knapp is intended as a college textbook in nonverbal communication. The book is 213 pages, well researched and annotated, an excellent survey of the field. It is certainly the best textbook treatment available on nonverbal communication.

Body Language and the Social Order and *How Behavior Means* by Albert E. Scheflen. *Body Language and the Social Order* has never been released in paperback (Prentice-Hall, 1972). Scheflen is a professor of psychiatry and is concerned primarily with the interpretation of nonverbal language. The book includes hundreds of pictures and interpretations of the nonverbal interaction taking place. *How Behavior Means* (Doubleday Anchor paperback, 1974) is a scholarly study of metacommunication, especially in the therapeutic process.

Nonverbal Communication (Harcourt Brace Jovanovich, School Department) by Louis Forsdale is a 162-page paperback for high school students. The book is a once-over-lightly that is interesting, but misses much of what is most important. If you are teaching a course in nonverbal communication, you might want to study an examination copy.

Silent Messages (Wadsworth Publishing) by Albert Mehrabian is a psychologist's look at both verbal and nonverbal communication. Mehrabian's concern is with "hidden" messages, whether verbal or nonverbal. The writing style is clear and reveals fine psychological insights.

Mannerisms of Speech and Gestures in Everyday Life (International Universities Press) by Sandor Feldman is a sort of dictionary of Freudian meanings behind speech mannerisms and common gestures. Fascinating but rather arbitrary and extremely Freudian.

Three Books by Erving Goffman: Strategic Interaction (Ballantine), *Interaction Ritual* (Doubleday Anchor) and *Relations in Public* (Basic Books) are three books by Erving Goffman on how people behave in public. Goffman is a "people-watcher" par excellence and is one of the big four nonverbal scientists (with Birdwhistell, Hall, and Sommer). Goffman's concern is with the rituals we go through to maintain the proper social behavior. His insights are among the most fascinating of any nonverbal researcher. Unfortunately Goffman's writing style includes lengthy footnotes that can drive a reader to despair. His style is quite difficult and will probably discourage all but the most avid high school students.

Kinesics and Context (Ballantine) by Ray Birdwhistell is one of the first scholarly books on kinesics to receive any sort of public attention. Although Birdwhistell is probably the most important writer on nonverbal language, he is also the most scholarly and difficult. His writing on kinesics is clear but demanding.

Nonverbal Communication: Readings with Commentary by Shirley Weitz (Oxford Press, 1974, hardcover or paperback) is a 350-page anthology of writings about nonverbal communication. All the big names in the field are represented in this book as well as many teachers and scholars who have never before appeared in a book. The tone is scholarly, but the choice of topics practical. Included are chapters on "The Doctor's Voice," "The Mother's Voice: Postdictor of Aspects of Her Baby's Behavior," "Territorial Defense and the Good Neighbor," and nineteen other articles.

3

A Primer in Mind Management:

Media Deception

IN THE FIRST chapter we saw that one of advertising's most effective deceptions is essentially the individual's self-deception — the common belief that ads influence other people, not oneself. This widespread assumption of personal invulnerability helps create the milieu in which ads can be effective persuaders. Two similar kinds of self-deception work in the mass media in general and enable it to be a force in mind management. One deception is the distinction people make between educational media and entertainment media; the other is the common belief that the mass media offer enough information to enable one to be well informed about national and world affairs.

Many media analysts argue that mass media do not have the power to manipulate minds, that the average person is not a malleable idiot ready to be told what to do by a twenty-one inch picture from New York. They are partly correct, but they base their arguments only on the attempts of the media to persuade. The contention here is that mass media are most effective as shapers of values when they entertain, not when they preach. The critics of media power often point out that newspaper endorsements of political candidates and money spent for media campaigns often have little measurable effect on the outcome of the election. But this argument does not deny the power of the media, it merely points out that people resist being told how to vote or what to think when they know someone is attempting to persuade them. This argument does not deal with the power of the media to influence values and attitudes when the audience has its "persuasion defenses" down.

In television, for example, there is a tendency to divide programming into two categories — educational items (public broadcasting, documentaries, cultural shows) and entertainment programs. This distinction causes media consumers to neglect the fact that *all programming is educational.*

In regard to news media the deceptive mind-set is that by following television newscasts and glancing through a local newspaper one can be considered well informed about local, national, and world affairs. The deception of being well informed in turn influences all further news consumption and leads to value judgments based on the incomplete facts. There is also a tendency in news consumption to distinguish between opinion news (editorials, journals of opinion, and interpretive news) and purely factual news (network news, newspapers, radio broadcasts). This distinction, like that between educational television and entertainment television, leads to neglect of the subtle biases found even in factual news.

In this chapter we will propose a way for students to examine the mind-managing aspects of entertainment programming on television and the criteria by which people judge themselves well informed about world affairs. The activities and readings suggested here leave plenty of room for students (and teachers) to draw their own conclusions about the content of the education.

THE EDUCATIONAL CONTENT OF ENTERTAINMENT PROGRAMMING

I recently watched a 1950 Lone Ranger television show in an audience of over two hundred educators. As an audience we learned a number of things from the viewing. First we learned that the Lone Ranger probably wore a mask because he was too embarrassed to allow his total lack of acting ability to show. We learned that dialogue written for television shows twenty-five years ago is today laughable (in fact the show was funnier than any current television comedy routine), and we learned that television of years past taught values that would be unacceptable today to many. The convoluted speech patterns of Tonto very likely gave many young viewers in the fifties an idea of what to expect from Indians but would today be branded as racist. This particular Lone Ranger episode also taught some rather strong ideas about what it takes to be a man that today's viewers could clearly see as education in the meaning of masculinity.

In the show we viewed Casper Dingle as a henpecked husband whose wife runs the ranch as well as Casper's life. The Lone Ranger enters the scene and gives the downtrodden husband a reluctant lesson in shooting, whereupon he turns into a "he-man." As the show ends Casper demands his wife make him some "grub," and when she objects, he pulls out his gun and waves it under her nose. He also proves his sudden lack of fear in the face of Ma Dingle by shooting her favorite vase to pieces. Thus the Lone Ranger is credited with the resurrection of Casper Dingle and with restoring the proper master-slave relationship in marriage.

Another 1950's television show, *That Man Bob,* was shown to the same audience and it too taught what is acceptable masculine and feminine behavior. In the episode, titled "How to Get a Woman," Bob Cummings tells his nephew how to trick his girl friend into helping him pay for a new carburetor for their car. Bob's trick is to paint the carburetor pink and tie a bow around it — of course the trick works. Later in the program Bob meets a woman with an exaggerated masculine personality and tricks her into becoming more "feminine" and therefore more able to be manipulated by men.

The audience for these two episodes could very clearly see the sexist "teaching" these two entertainment shows contained. When the shows were originally telecast, the teaching content was not questioned because viewers considered them merely entertainment. The 1975 audience was far enough removed from the television shows to see their propaganda content clearly and to realize that today's shows very likely have the same kind of education content although with different messages. But the education content of contemporary entertainment is more difficult to recognize.

Entertainment media are, to borrow Erik Barnouw's phrase, "propaganda for the status quo." But to see the propaganda inherent in entertainment requires the development of a new kind of vision.

Following is a series of worksheets to use in developing that new kind of vision. To use them requires intense concentration while watching television. They are best used with groups who can compile dozens of worksheets and then combine them into cumulative studies representing long periods of time, many programs, and all the local channels and the three networks.

The objective of the worksheets is not to bring about certain conclusions about which values television teaches, although students will certainly reach some conclusions. The objective is rather to teach the kind of vision that can see entertainment as an influence upon values and attitudes.

Sex Roles Analysis

The "Sex Role Analysis Worksheet" is best used by having each person note only characters of one sex. The worksheet should be used to investigate the image of both man and woman on entertainment television. In this sheet both the program and the ads that pay for the program are monitored.

(Permission is hereby granted for teachers to reproduce these worksheets for in-classroom use only.)

Drawing Conclusions

1. A NOW study (see reading list on page 68) found that in television commercials 16.7 percent of the women were used as sex objects, 17.1 percent were presented as unintelligent, and 42.6 percent were household functionaries. How does this compare with your findings?

2. From your monitoring of television shows what kind of woman is the most likely to be found on television? What kind of man?

3. What distortions of reality does television introduce into the male/female image?

4. Examine the credits that are shown for each television program and determine if both males and females are well represented among those who make television shows. Ignore the credits for the cast of characters and concentrate on the technicians and the people who create the show.

SEX ROLE ANALYSIS

DATE	TIMES	NETWORK		List all males or all females who appear WHICH SEX STUDIED		
PROGRAM OR	PRODUCT ADV.	Approx. Age	Name or some description of character (List each person once)	Occupation (if known)	Summary of what person does or what qualities he or she is shown as possessing

5. What conclusions can be drawn from the study?

Readings in Sex Roles in Media

The following readings are recommended to assist in reaching conclusions and developing a new vision:

* * *

"Are TV Commercials Insulting to Women? Good Housekeeping Readers Say NO by a Slim Majority," in *Good Housekeeping* of May 1971.

* * *

"NOW Says TV Commercials Insult Women," by Judith Adler Hennessee and Joan Nichols in *The New York Times Magazine* of May 28, 1972. These two articles offer competing views of women in commercials. The NOW article could help in preparing the worksheet.

* * *

"What's Television doing for 51% of the Population?" by Caroline Bird in *TV Guide* of February 27, 1971.

* * *

"Women: Correcting the Myths," by Midge Kovacs in *The New York Times* of August 26, 1972.

* * *

"Are Little Girls Being Harmed by 'Sesame Street?'" by Jane Bergman in *The New York Times* of January 2, 1972, section II, page 13.

Sport as Education

Of all forms of mass entertainment one would think that sports would contain the least amount of education and the highest degree of

A Primer in Mind Management

pure entertainment. But sport itself is an expression of the values of a society and when sport is presented on television, an even greater educational load is placed on it.

Watch a sports contest on television and listen for the ways sport educates during your viewing. The worksheet following will suggest some of these.

Readings in Sport as Education

Super Spectator and the Electric Lilliputians by William O. Johnson (Little, Brown, 1971) is a nicely written book about the impact of television on sports. The influences of television sport on the nation is best examined in chapter one. If this book is not available in your area, try "TV Made it all a New Game" by the same author in *Sports Illustrated* of December 29, 1969.

* * *

"Sport is a Three-Letter Word," by Lowell Powell in *University of Chicago Magazine,* March/April 1974. Powell sees sports not as a spectator show but as a way to learn about ourselves, express ourselves, and enjoy a healthy body. He comments, "When people confine sports to running between the refrigerator and the TV set, we're in trouble."

* * *

Esquire of October 1974 is entirely devoted to sport and includes a number of potentially useful articles including "Media Re-examined," a profile of ABC-TV producer Roone Arledge, and an article on the influence of film on sports and vice versa.

Drawing Conclusions

1. Are blacks (or any other minority group) presented in a realistic manner on television? To answer this question fully you must also consider, "Are whites presented in a realistic manner on television?"

2. In what ways does television contribute to stereotyped presentations of minorities?

THE MESSAGE OF A SPORTSCAST

DURING THE TELECAST	AFTER THE TELECAST
List each product advertised. (If the same product is advertised more than once, indicate it.)	Why was this product advertised during this time? What qualities in a sports fan might also make the fan a potential buyer of the product?
Any time an announcer characterizes an athlete note the word or phrase used (courageous, rugged, tough, etc.) | Positive | Negative |	Judging from the lists on the left side of this page, is there a tendency to describe athletes in larger-than-life terms? What other conclusions can be drawn from the lists?
List any words used by the announcers that also have a military meaning (bomb, rifle, squad, attack, etc.)	

BLACKS ON PRIME TIME

EACH CHART FOR ONE PRIME-TIME EVENING ON ONE NETWORK   NETWORK   TIMES

Name of program or product advertised	Role, function or occupation of blacks who appear (List each individual once only)	What does this person accomplish during the program	Rate this person in terms of believability: 1. unreal 2. not too real 3. fairly real 4. highly real	Sex	Approximate age

3. What conclusions can you draw based on your own observations of television programs?

Readings About Blacks on Television

"The New Stereotypes are No Better Than the Old" by Roger Wareham and Peter C. Byone in *The Urban Review* of November/December 1972. Wareham and Byone conclude that "The characters and situations the black performers have to depict are nearly always representations of what whites conceive a black hero should be."

* * *

"Media Myths on Violence," by Terry Ann Knopf from *Columbia Journalism Review,* Spring 1970. This article deals with the distortions of reality introduced by the news media in regard to blacks and violence. "We have all grown so used to viewing blacks as stereotyped criminals that it is difficult to picture them in any other role; hence such frequent press concoctions as 'roving gangs,' 'roving vandals' . . . ."

* * *

Freedomways: A Quarterly Review of the Freedom Movement (799 Broadway, Suite 542, New York, NY 10003) devoted an entire issue (number three of volume fourteen) to the image of blacks in the mass media. Included in the issue are articles on "The Rise and Falls of Blacks in Serious Television," "Black Shows for White Viewers," and about a dozen others. The issue also includes a 228-item bibliography on blacks in the media.

Drawing Conclusions

1. How does the number of ads on Saturday morning television compare with that on prime-time adult television?

2. Are children's programs (a) less violent, (b) more violent, or (c) equally as violent as adult fare?

3. Is there a general educational message of Saturday morning television?

KIDVID

To be completed during one Saturday morning children's programming on one net | Net | Date

THE PROGRAMS

Name of program	Note each act of violence	What does the program "teach"?

THE COMMERCIALS

List each product	If food — list main ingredient*	If toy — give price	What sales appeal is used?

During the time I watched there was one commercial every _____ minutes. The most commonly advertised products were:

*Look for this information on package label in a grocery store if needed

4. What conclusions can you reach about the ads? What is the most common product type advertised?

5. What kind of food is the most advertised? Go to a grocery store to read ingredient labels if needed, but find out what the two main ingredients are of all food advertised on children's television on one Saturday morning.

6. Do you find children's advertising fair or do you consider it a form of taking advantage of young minds?

Readings About Children's Television

"TV for Kiddies. Truth, Goodness, Beauty and a Little Bit of Brainwash," by Robert Liebert and Rita Poulos in *Psychology Today* of November 1972. One study quoted in this article observes that "when Eastern children, especially those from urban areas, vacation in the West, they often expect ranch hands to behave like the cowboys they have seen so often in Westerns on TV and at the movies . . ."

* * *

"Outrage of Children's Television," by Gene Shalit in *Ladies' Home Journal* of January 1973.

* * *

"Is TV Brutalizing Your Child?" by Eliot Daley in *Look* of December 2, 1969. According to Daley, "Between the ages of 5 and 14, your children and mine may, if they are average viewers, witness the annihilation of 12,000 human beings."

* * *

"How to Win Friends and Influence Kids on Television" by Marilyn Elias in *Human Behavior* of April 1974 studies the use of motivational research in kidvid advertising. Because children demand specific products and brands at the supermarket, mothers spend an average of $1.66 more per week shopping. Thus Junior contributes $1.5 billion to the boom in grocery-store sales.

* * *

The Early Window: Effects of Television on Children and Youth by Robert Liebert, John Neale, and Emily Davidson (Pergamon Press, Elmsford, NY, 1973) is a scholarly yet highly readable book on television's influence on society through children. The book is part of a general psychology series and draws on experimental studies of the children-television confrontation in relation to both violence and advertising. The book goes far beyond looking at television and children as it considers television as a window to the world, "a school if you will, through which the child first perceives his society and then learns from repeated examples to cope with the vicissitudes of living." Highly recommended.

* * *

Action for Children's Television is a citizen action group with local chapters throughout the country (some supply speakers). They have a newsletter, a free resource list, a paperback called *Action for Children's Television* (Avon). They also have a film, *But First This Message* (rental $25, sale $100, 15 minutes), which contains clips from kidvid shows, accompanied by comments from professional television observers and children themselves.

Drawing Conclusions

1. Which is the most violent show currently on the air?
2. Why does television feature violence as a regular part of its entertainment programming?
3. What do people learn from violent television shows?
4. Based on your observations, how many deaths does the average viewer (assume two hours a day of television-watching is average) see in a lifetime?
5. Complete: On CBS during prime time there is one violent act committed every ___ minutes. On NBC there is one every ___ minutes and on ABC there is one violent act every ___ minutes.
6. What is the most common reason for violence on the programs?

VIDEO VIOLENCE

Put together enough charts to cover all three networks for a one-week period. Watch only prime time.

Label each line as a 10-minute period during prime time, e.g. 7:40 - 7:50, 7:50 - 8:00	Program	List by name any weapons shown. Indicate how many if more than one	Night watched Describe each violent act that takes place — (knifing, shooting, fist fight, threat to shoot, etc.)	Network Count of deaths. Indicate sex of each victim	Reason for violent act

Readings on Media Violence

"Violence on TV: Why People are Upset," in October 29, 1973, *U.S. News and World Report.*

* * *

Television and Growing Up: The Impact of Televised Violence is a United Public Health Service Report to the Surgeon General. This 280-page report is available for $2.25 from the U.S. Government Printing Office, Washington, DC 20402. According to this report, "The evidence does indicate that televised violence may lead to increased aggressive behavior in certain subgroups of children, who might constitute a small portion or a substantial proportion of the total population of young television viewers." The report also finds that "The heavy viewers of violence are disproportionately clustered among males over 50 years old and among males with less than a full high school education."

* * *

"TV Violence *Is* Harmful" by Jesse Steinfeld, M.D., in *Reader's Digest,* April 1973, argues that " we can no longer tolerate the high level of violence that saturates children's television."

* * *

To Establish Justice, To Insure Domestic Tranquility is the title of the Bantam paperback edition of the Report of the National Commission on the Causes and Prevention of Violence. Chapter 8 of that report, "Violence in Television Entertainment" is an excellent summary of television violence as a value-shaper.

* * *

Violence and the Mass Media, edited by Otto N. Larsen (Harper & Row, 1968) is the best collection of writings about media violence. The book covers all the media and includes technical studies as well as popular writing. Parts II and IV relate most directly to the worksheets.

CRIME AND THE CRIMINAL

USE THIS WORKSHEET ONLY FOR PROGRAMS IN WHICH CRIME IS INVOLVED.

Program	Nature of each crime committed	What kind of person is the victim?	Is the criminal punished? How?	Description of criminal — Age / Sex / Race

A Primer in Mind Management

Drawing Conclusions

1. Find out which crimes are most commonly committed in the United States. (An almanac might have this information or consult with a reference librarian.) Find out what percentage of crimes reported are solved. Compare both of these answers to the television version of crime in our society.

2. Was there any crime shown on television in which corporations were presented as engaging in criminal behavior?

3. According to Joseph Dominick (see reading listed on next page), "TV crime appears to be a white collar occupation committed primarily by specialists or by people with middle-class occupations." He also found that "no one under 20 got busted and nonwhites comprised only 7 percent of those who did." Do the observations reflected on your worksheets agree with these findings?

4. What do crime shows on television teach about crime and criminals?

Readings About Crime and Criminals

"According to the Mass Media It's Not Crime" by Robert Cirino is chapter 18 in his book *Don't Blame the People* (see page 97). Cirino comments on the news media's lack of coverage of organized crime. Compare Cirino's findings about news coverage to network entertainment programming.

* * *

"Staked Out in Hollywood," by John Fleischman in the December 1973 issue of *Human Behavior* examines how television and movie cops compare to reality. Fleischman's article is entertaining, but does raise questions like, "Should we really go on watching actors impersonating the way other actors have always impersonated policemen? Are we in the process of fabricating a police myth via television that will last for decades to come?"

* * *

"Crime and Law Enforcement on Prime-Time Television" by Joseph R.

Dominick in *Public Opinion Quarterly,* Summer 1973 (Vol. 37, No. 2, pages 241ff). Dominick compares television crime to real crime and finds that the two are hardly similar. According to Dominick, the television criminal is a "one-dimensional caricature who might get lost in a line-up of Sunday school teachers."

Readings About Television, Lifestyle, and Problem-Solving

"Social Comment and TV Censorship" by David Dempsey in *Saturday Review* of July 12, 1969. Dempsey finds that "millions of Americans find prime-time entertainment a nostalgic sanctuary — perhaps the only one left — where few men swear, everyone is politically neutral, the church is never criticized, men and women do not live together out of wedlock, the happy ending is assured, the criminal brought to trial, and the little disturbances of life are usually resolved in favor of the status quo."

* * *

"A Heartwarming New TV Season From the Same Folks Who Brought You Law and Order" by Dick Hobson is a fine article on entertainment programming and their values in the October 1974 issue of *Human Behavior.* "CBS had done research to prove that audiences didn't like three things: people from New York, people with mustaches and people who were divorced." Quoting producer Quinn Martin: "We're hitting the great heartland of America, and they want shows where the leading man does something positive and has a positive result. Every time you go against that, you can almost automatically say you are going to fail."

* * *

"Test Pattern for Living," by Nicholas Johnson in *Saturday Review* of May 29, 1971. "Not only do commercials and programs explicitly preach materialism, conspicuous consumption, status consciousness, sexploitation, and fantasy worlds of quick, shallow solutions, but even the settings and subliminal messages are commercials for the consumption style of life." Johnson's book *Test Pattern for Living* is also highly recommended

LIFESTYLE AND PROBLEM-SOLVING

Watch one evening of prime-time television on one network.　　Date:　　　　　Time:

Programs watched:

Problems faced by leading characters	Means used to solve the problem

Occupation of each character	Do the living conditions of each character fit the occupation (e.g., a maid who owns a house would probably not be fitting, a doctor in a mansion would)?

Make some conclusion about the problems, solutions, and lifestyles shown on prime-time television in regard to what they teach about life.

for this study. Since it was published in paperback only (Bantam), it might be difficult to locate.

* * *

"Television Pollutes Us All," by Loring Mandel from *The New York Times* of March 25, 1970. Mandel examines some of the "lies" that TV teaches including: "That any means are justifiable. That passivity is wise. That intensity is a spectator sport. That people bleed only from the corner of the mouth, and that instant regeneration of human tissue is a fact of violence. And by the purposeful omission of material that is relevant to our contemporary situation the entertainment programmers make reality more foreign to us."

SOAP OPERA ANALYSIS

Watch one soap opera for at least one week and make conclusions based on the following observations:

What kinds of women are shown?
What kinds of problems are they faced with solving?
How are their problems solved?
What kinds of men appear most often in soap operas?
In what ways are the soap operas true to life?
In what ways are they missing part of life?

Readings About Soap Operas and Values

"The Trauma of TV's Troubled Soap Families," by M. L. Ramsdell in *Family Coordinator* of July 1973. If this magazine is not available, the article is summarized in *Human Behavior* of January 1974, page 62. Ramsdell watched six hundred hours of soap operas and concludes that their message is " the 'good life' can be achieved by anybody who is a white male professional or white female who marries the professional and, subsequently becomes a mommy."

* * *

The Soaps by Madeleine Edmondson and David Rounds is a book (Stein and Day, 1974) about soap operas. Best chapters for help in seeing the message of the soaps are "Soapscape" and "The Soap Watchers." The authors begin by quoting James Thurber's definition of a soap opera as ". . . a kind of sandwich, whose recipe is simple enough, although it took years to compound. Between thick slices of advertising, spread twelve minutes of dialogue, add predicament, villainy, and female suffering in equal measure, throw in a dash of nobility, sprinkle with tears, season with organ music, cover with a rich announcer sauce, and serve five times a week."

* * *

"The Soaps – Anything but 99 and 44/100 Percent Pure" by Edith Efron in *TV Guide* of March 13, 1965, complains that the shows reflect only the sickest side of female sexuality.

* * *

"Everything's Up-to-Date in Soap Operas" by Marya Mannes in *TV Guide* of March 15, 1969, examines soaps and unreality.

* * *

"Mainlining Soaps: The Allure of Daytime Television Drama," by Stephen West in *Popular Psychology* of September 1972. West points out that one theory which explains the success of the soaps is "that women tune in soap operas to watch someone who has more misery than she does. It makes you feel good to discover that somebody else has it worse."

THE CONTENT OF THE NEWS MEDIA

The supermarket grocery shelves and the nation's news media have something in common. Both offer a dazzling array of cleverly packaged products, both provide the illusion of a great diversity of choice and both require careful study on the part of the consumer to obtain the best value for the time and money spent.

Increasingly bulky daily newspapers, longer national television news, local television newscasts up to an hour each evening with another thirty minutes later in the night and all-news radio stations contribute to the belief that there is an abundance of news. That we are flooded with news as part of an "information explosion" has become a readily accepted cliché.

Surveys reveal that most adults consider themselves "well-informed about the affairs of the nation and the world." Yet a regularly taken Roper poll that asks, "From where do you obtain most of your information about the world?" has found the percentage of people who reply, "Television" has been increasing steadily over the past decade. The latest poll found that well over sixty percent of the respondents chose television over other media as their prime source of information. These two facts are difficult to reconcile since even a casual study of television news reveals it is only a headline service and not a source of information enabling one to shape a worldview.

The ideas in this section are designed to help students see that television and newspaper provide less news than might be expected, that much of what is presented as news is propaganda and that there is a wide choice of information sources available in the form of more specialized media.

How Much News Do TV and Newspapers Provide?

Thirty-minute newscasts and thick papers help create the illusion of a wealth of news. But a closer inspection reveals the main content of a newspaper is not news and a surprisingly small amount of a typical thirty-minute newscast actually gives information. To illustrate this point it is best to allow students to make this discovery on their own using local media. The following two worksheets require a bit of calculation and time to complete, but will give exact answers measuring the amount of news. The television chart should be used to measure both national network news and the output of the local stations. Using only one day's newspaper (or television news) will give approximate answers although a week of news gives a more accurate picture.

ANALYSIS OF THE USE OF SPACE IN A NEWSPAPER

Paper: Date: Total No. of Pages:

To obtain an accurate count use a column inch as a basic measurement. A column inch is one column wide and one inch deep. For a less accurate but quicker measurement estimate in terms of half-columns; a half-column is one column wide and one half page deep.

Amount of paper devoted to advertising: _____%

Amount of paper devoted to news: _____%

Amount of paper devoted to non-advertising and non-news: _____%
   (Agree before beginning this worksheet what kind of
   material is non-news and non-advertising.)

What percentage of news is local reporting? _____%

What percentage of news is from AP and UPI? _____%

Draw some conclusions about news coverage in the paper:

Students are generally surprised when they discover that newspapers contain more advertising than news. Fat newspapers contribute to the idea of an information explosion. When Winston Churchill visited the United States after the war he reportedly was asked what he thought of American papers. He replied, "Your toilet paper is too thin and your newspapers are too thick." Since Churchill made that remark newspapers have become even thicker.

In 1950 the average daily paper was 34 pages. in 1970 the average was up to 54 pages but contained a smaller percentage of news. In those twenty years the news consumer did get a bit more news, measured in column inches. But according to a study conducted by journalist Ben Bagdikian, the increase in news was largely "journalistic junk — euphoric mush about real estate, food, fashions and 'special sections' whose unpaid space is mainly or all public relations for the advertisers to give readers the impression that they are still looking at a newspaper." Eighty-three percent of the additional pages gained from 1950 to 1970 was advertising and most of the remaining seventeen percent was news of the public-relations puffery type.

In 1970 the average daily newspaper contained 37 columns of news (defining news as everything except ads, headlines and art). The average paper first counts the amount of advertising paid for and then tells the news editor how many columns are left for news — on an average this amounts to forty percent of the total space in the newspaper.

In completing the worksheet compare the statistics among all the local papers. If there are neighborhood or suburban papers in your area, calculate their news content also. Decide which paper provides the most news.

To determine if the amount of news provided by local papers has increased over the years consult papers from five and ten years ago in the library or newspaper office.

Before completing the worksheets discuss with students what should be counted as news and make sure everyone knows how to perform the measurement.

The percentage of news from the wire services (AP, UPI) also surprises students in some cities. On some smaller papers the total newshole is filled with wire release material and press releases. If AP and UPI were to cease operation the information explosion for some news consumers would turn immediately into a famine.

The television news analysis sheet will require teamwork to compile accurately. The sheet demands careful timing and quick writing. The best approach to gathering data for the chart is to allow those who watched the same newscast to compare notes and iron out differences in timings and judgments. Groups can also compare timings for the different networks and for the local news of competing stations to make comparative news judgments.

The most common result of this study is that students find out which television station locally gives the most news. They also often conclude that the three networks are quite similar in coverage. They are also graphically taught that less than half of an average thirty-minute newscast is devoted to actual news. My own spot check on a local CBS outlet showed that its 10 o'clock news contained 8 minutes 40 seconds of

A Primer in Mind Management

ANALYSIS OF TV NEWSCASTS			
Date:	Time:	Station or network:	
Use a stopwatch or watch with accurate second hand for this sheet.			
Type of content		Amount of time in seconds	% of entire newscast
HARD NEWS (world, national & local events of importance)			
SOFT NEWS (humor, entertainment items, human interest, trivia)			
SPORTS			
WEATHER			
ADVERTISING			
MISCELLANEOUS ("patter," credits, introduction, editorials)			
Identify each news item:	Total No. of stories _____ Average time given to each _____ Conclusion about newscast viewed:		

news and 9 minutes 45 seconds of ads and slightly more than 3 minutes each of weather, commentary, and sports.

These are points to consider after the statistics on the worksheets are compiled: Why is so much time devoted to the weather? Which local station best covers local news? Which network gives the most national news? Which station (or network) gives the most in-depth coverage and which gives the greatest number of stories? Do TV stations have something that compares to puffery in the newspapers? Does newspaper or television give the most details about a news happening? Do you think that people who watch television news are well informed about events (a) locally, (b) in the nation, (c) in the rest of the world?

Propaganda Disguised as News

Much of what passes for news, for factual reporting and pure information, is really an attempt to persuade the audience by managing the flow of information. The government and its various agencies spend more money to influence public opinion than the three television networks combined. Professional organizations employ skilled publicists to flood newspapers, radio and television stations with press releases extolling the virtues of their clients.

Not all managed news is useless — this is often the means that news media use to find out about events and future happenings. But a press release written by a professional public-relations person or by the organization that makes the "news" is understandably biased.

One of the best ways to help students recognize managed news is to post in class examples of press releases obtained from the school office or parents of students. After reading a number of releases, the kind of language used (press-release English) becomes readily recognizable when presented as news.

While doing this, find as many examples as possible of propaganda news in the local papers. The real estate, fashion, food, and travel sections are the best sources for the most obvious examples.

Students should also be taught to recognize *pseudo-events* — happenings created for the media by people who have something to sell or who stand to gain by convincing the public of a particular viewpoint. Examples of pseudo-events include many press conferences, speeches, prepared interviews, demonstrations, publicity stunts, and some public ceremonies. Politicians readily agree to fly halfway across the country to address a group of a few hundred people not because of the value of communicating to these people but because the news media will be present to extend his or her thoughts throughout the community and perhaps the nation.

One criterion to apply in deciding if an item is a pseudo-event or not is to ask, "Would this be happening if the news media did not exist?" If the answer is no, the event was tailor-made to gain time and space in the news media and can very likely be classified as a pseudo-event.

After students can easily identify press-release news in special sections of the newspaper, have them look more closely in the main section for pseudo-events and the attempts of political figures to get their opinions in the news.

Alternatives to Mass Media News

If there is one message of this brief unit in mind management, it is that in order to be even close to well-informed one needs to do more than watch television news and glance through the paper.

What the "more" includes can be suggested by bringing into the classroom (perhaps with the cooperation of the local library) examples of magazines and papers that provide news coverage in greater depth. Such publications tend to be far more opinionated and biased than either television news or newspapers. Perhaps it is not possible to go beyond a mere reporting of the surface facts without exposing one's own biases and opinions.

Magazines such as *The New Republic, The Nation, New Times, New York,* and news weeklies, *Saturday Review* and scores of others (including many so-called "underground" publications) should be explored by a class. Also make available to students papers such as *The Christian Science Monitor, National Observer, The Wall Street Journal,* and the closest thing we have to a national paper — *The New York Times.*

One assignment that will help students realize the complexity and diversity of news is to have each one select a news story of national importance from the local paper. Each then finds articles or news stories about that same subject in at least six other publications, reads them, points out biases, draws conclusions, and follows future news items about the event in the paper.

RESOURCE GUIDE FOR
THE STUDY OF MIND MANAGEMENT

Films

Television and Politics (25 minutes, color, BFA Educational Media, 2211 Michigan Avenue, Santa Monica, CA 90404) is an excerpt from Mike Wallace's CBS-TV show *60 Minutes*. The 1970 film has the high quality that was a *60 Minutes* trademark and a topic that is both timely and crucial.

The film could well be called "How to Sell a Candidate," or "Buying Votes with Ads." Political spots are shown beginning with those of Harry Truman in 1948, through the clever *March-of-Time* commercial for Eisenhower in 1952. Nixon's almost legendary "Checkers Speech," is shown as is Kefauver's use of Eisenhower's own commercials in 1956, the 1960 Kennedy-Nixon debates, and finally Barry Goldwater's 1964 television spots that made ads for political candidates on television a lethal weapon. The film clips are damning, revealing, embarrassing, and often humorous.

After tracing the recent history of the political ad the film switches to interviews with the people who market the candidates. Wallace asks Hubert Humphrey's packager about the morality of a spot in which Agnew is shown on screen and the sound track consists entirely of a man laughing. The media man claims to be concerned about politics, not government, and views himself as a "gun for hire."

Wallace and some of those interviewed question the economics and morality of television campaigns. Agnew's media man says, "We want our candidate to be liked more than understood, we're reaching for the heart rather than the mind." There are surprisingly frank interviews with political and communications industry people. The film is very much concerned with media morality and even more basically with a Brave New World use of the media in politics.

I. F. Stone's Weekly (62 minutes, B&W, I.F. Stone Project, P.O. Box 315, Franklin Lakes, NJ 07407) should be shown to all students of mass media in the hope that it might inspire the reporters of tomorrow to emulate the clarity, toughness, official skepticism, and humility of Isadore Feinstein Stone.

I. F. Stone is an investigative newsman who started his own newsletter in response to a McCarthy-era blacklisting. *I. F. Stone's Weekly* grew to a 1969 circulation of 70,000 when Stone finally retired at the age of sixty-four. Today he writes occasional pieces for *The New York Review of Books*.

Stone's first assumption is that "every government is run by liars," his second is that "a government always reveals a great deal if you really take the trouble to study what it says." Newspapers that print largely what is given out by "official sources" act as the unwitting propaganda arm of the government. While Stone talks about establishment reporters and the purpose of the media as "merchandising," the film shows a few seconds of tennis between then press secretary Ron Ziegler and an ABC reporter. The private White House courts appear inviting and even Tricia Nixon looks on smilingly. With this transposing of sight and sound the film places viewers in the position of the common barnyard animals near the end of *Animal Farm* who sneak a peek into the dinner between the farmers and the ruling pigs, only to notice it has become difficult to distinguish the pigs from the people.

The sound of I. F. Stone's uncluttered truth is often placed in opposition to the on-camera lies of a Johnson, Nixon, or McNamara. Stone printed the truth about the Tonkin Gulf incident days after it happened while the rest of the press simply repeated government statements. Because Stone was rejected by official Washington, he dug his truth, available to any reporter with two eyes and an open mind, from the avalanche of government documents and newspaper reports.

Stone is no wild-eyed radical; his appearance is more that of an antihero and his rhetoric is delivered more with a passion for truth than a hatred for liars. He is living testimony that one person with limited resources can be important to a nation.

The film was made by Jerry Bruck over a three-year period in a cinéma vérité style, which often has a homemade look. He managed to take a visually unexciting subject and produce an important and engrossing documentary.

A Special Report (17 minutes, B&W, University of Southern California, Film Distribution Library, Department of Cinema, University Park, Los Angeles, CA 90007) is a satire about the fascination of television news with violent death. In it Robert Rancor presents a special report for "Channel Three Moment News" on the brutal murder of Candy Parabola, a twenty-two-year-old topless dancer.

Using all the cliché camera shots and narration of a television "special report" the film tells how the murder happened as "the curvaceous lady moved quietly in the privacy of her own home." There are the inevitable interviews with a neighbor who says, "She was a nice girl," and the police inspector who casually says it was "probably just your typical irritations killing," and the reporter comments that "she was a symptom of the disease of violence."

Each time a new character appears an identifying tag is superimposed on the screen. CANDY PARABOLA — VICTIM and NEGRO POLICE INSPECTOR are two that make viewers aware of the danger of these all-too-compact labels flashed so routinely on the screen.

The reporter wraps up the special report by quoting Shakespeare while standing in a cemetery. *A Special Report* is wacky yet incisive. It deals with the dangers involved in the media's handling of crime, and their tendency to label and to sound profound while saying nothing. It captures perfectly the ability of a medium to use the guise of public service to play a titilating striptease (will they show the body?) with a frightened yet blood-hungry audience.

Television News: Measure of a Medium (16 minutes, color, BFA Educational Media, 2211 Michigan Avenue, Santa Monica, CA 90704) takes a look at the reliability of televised news. Part One is a typical instructional film, adequate but never really exciting. Four working newsmen talk about the special problems posed by television. One newscaster even admits that a television news show equals, by actual word count, only two-thirds of one newspaper page. The four discuss the problems of balance, time, and news sources and give a defense of charges that TV news is biased and distorted.

The second part of *Measure of a Medium* enables the film to earn its rental fee. Two versions of the same news story, about conditions at the local jail, are shown as they might have appeared on a six o'clock newscast. Both filmed reports are realistic and seem very much like what passes for news on most stations. Students are asked to stop viewing the film and discuss the differences in both versions. The first filmed report turns out to be a subtle and highly believable example of distortion by omission, the second is far more complete and honest. Yet without a comparison either seems like the whole truth. This comparison is a fine use of film and raises the film above the level of being merely a discussion starter.

Gaines "Sixteen" Films Company (15207 Stagg Street, Van Nuys, CA 91405) sells 16 mm prints of old television shows. A recent listing offered a *Let's Make a Deal* show for $9.75 (this is a sale price, not rental), *Newlywed Game* for $9.75, and lots of *Dr. Hudson's Secret Journal.* Gaines also sells television commercials, but they are not listed in every catalog. The available films are listed in a monthly publication; a single copy is free although a $4.00-a-year subscription charge is the norm.

Organizations

American Council for Better Broadcasts (111 King Street, Madison WI 53703) is a nonprofit organization which aims to "improve by educational means the quality of radio and television." They publish a newsletter called *Better Broadcasts News*, and have a number of publications of use to teachers available. Write for a sample newsletter and description of their other activities.

American Research Bureau (4320 Ammendale Road, Beltsville, MD 20705) offers a number of publications free to teachers in single copies. A wall map, "U. S. Television Market ADI's," shows "Areas of Dominant Interest," (ADI's). Also *Television Market Area Survey Guide* shows how often each market is rated. *Estimates of U.S. TV Households* shows how many people in each county and state have television. *Exclusive Television Market Areas of Dominant Influence in the U.S.* gives statistics for each of the ADI's, listing the counties that make up each ADI, the rank according to number of television households, television penetration in each, and the total number of estimated television households and the number of men, women, teens, and children in the ADI.

Television Information Office (745 Fifth Avenue, New York, NY 10022) is an organization supported by the three networks, individual television stations, and the National Association of Broadcasters to act as a sort of public-relations arm for the industry. The information it supplies is shaped by the need to present television favorably. The TIO is a nice balancing source of information to use with the easily available television criticism. They have a list of free and inexpensive publications, some of which are excellent and useful in the high school class.

A.C. Nielsen Company, the ratings people, have a number of publications and a film available free to educators.

Two booklets are available in classroom quantity. "Neilsen Television '75" (updated yearly) is a colorful presentation of graphs and charts illustrating the vital statistics of American TV usage. It is a useful handout for a television study. The other booklet available in bulk upon request is "What the Ratings Really Mean."

Available in single copies upon request is a demonstration of a Nielsen rating report — ask for "NSI Demonstration Report." Also ask for a complete list of other publications.

The free-loan film titled *Nielsen Television Index* explains the Nielsen rating system. Request film or publications from Promotion Department, A.C. Nielsen Company, Nielsen Plaza, Northbrook, IL 60062.

Books

News From Nowhere: Television and the News by Edward Jay Epstein (Random House, 1973) proposes that the shaping factor of television news is the economic and corporate needs of the producing network. Although I find Epstein's theory unproven after three hundred pages and his study far from objective, I did find his behind-the-scenes account of how news is born for network TV both entertaining and instructive.

To counter the common belief that all network newscasts are basically the same, Epstein offers statistics to show that only twelve percent of all news stories are covered by all three networks.

To support his theory that news is a dramatic program, Epstein offers a fascinating 1963 memorandum from Reuven Frank, then executive producer of the NBC evening news stating, "Every news story should without any sacrifice of probity or responsibility, display the attributes of fiction, of drama. It should have structure and conflict, problem and denouement, rising action and falling action, a beginning, a middle and an end. These are not only the essentials of drama; they are the essentials of narrative."

Epstein makes a strong case for television news as a sort of visual headline service with stories selected from AP and UPI wires — seventy percent of all network television news items originate with the wire services. He points out that television correspondents are generalists who are expected to know little about the subject on which they report and who do so much traveling that they have little time for professional newsgathering or investigation.

While writing his book Epstein was allowed to sit in on NBC news meetings and was given free rein to observe the news operations. Such inside observation results in interesting reading about a subject shrouded in mystery yet used by most people as their primary source of news information. *News from Nowhere* is seriously flawed but still one of the most instructive books available about television news.

About Television by Martin Mayer (Harper & Row, 1972, 433 pages) is one of the most readable books available about television. Mayer plays the role of the guide taking readers behind the scenes and screens of televisionland. He plays his role with fitting objectivity, leaving criticism of television for others.

In highly readable prose he explains which programs draw which kinds of viewers, the difference between American and European television, how advertisers buy television time, the contrasting views of networks and public television, how a television show is put together, Monday Night Football, the fairness doctrine, and on and on for more than four hundred pages. Reading level is suitable for high school.

The Age of Television by Leo Bogart (Frederick Ungar Publishing Co., NY, third edition, 1972, 513 pages) is *the* place to go for statistics about television. Be sure to have the third edition for the updated charts and statistics it contains. Much of this book goes back to the fifties and is dated but it still is the best single collection of statistics on American viewing habits. A reference book rather than bedtime reading.

Coping With Television by Joseph Littell (McDougal, Littell & Co., Box

1667, Evanston, IL 60204, 213 pages) is the only collection of readings about television expressly designed for high school students. There are well-chosen selections about the impact of television on society, cable television, educational television, the FCC, television production, program formats, news, the image of women, minorities, children's shows, violence on television, ratings, television commercials, and television in government and politics.

Being There by Jerry Kosinski (Bantam Books, 1970, 118 pages) is very likely the most important contemporary work of literature dealing with the social effects of television. Television has yet to inspire much fiction with the exception of a few poems and science fiction stories.

Being There is a parable about Chance, a retarded gardener shut off from the outside world, depending for nurture on his garden and the television. From the tube he learns how people act and what the world is like. When his rich employer dies, Chance is thrown into the world for the first time. Purely by accident he meets a wealthy, powerful man. Chance's simpleness, silence, and his constant references to gardening present a "cool" image and lead people to see in him what they will. They regard his garden talk as a subtle metaphor and he becomes a national celebrity and even a political candidate.

As a parable the book is a rich mine of insights into the media world. The parable asks can "being there" on the television screen provide enough identity to guide one to power and success? The value of *Being There* is that it is fine literature as well as a bit of media anthropology.

The Crowd-Catchers: Introducing Television by Robert Lewis Shayon (Saturday Review Press, 1973, 150 pages) is as succinct and basic an introduction to television as can be read. The book demands a motivated reader and is unlikely to be popular as a high school text but should prove useful in college. For media and television teachers the book is close to a "must."

Shayon's Crowd-Catchers are the television station and network owners. It is their job to capture audiences and sell them to sponsors. In tracing the history of television, Shayon concentrates on ownership of the media outlets to explain why television today is controlled by the few to sell consumer goods to the multitudes.

Shayon briefly treats the technical aspects of how television works; he looks at television in other countries, at the economics of telecasting, its failure to serve the public, and its future. His final plea and hope for television is that "We must all become TV producers, knowledgeable with camera and tape." His argument is that television must change from a passive medium to one in which all citizens can participate.

Don't Blame the People: How the News Media Use Bias, Distortion and Censorship to Manipulate Public Opinion by Robert Cirino. (Vintage paperback) The author is a high school journalism teacher, seemingly obsessed with showing exactly what the subtitle of his book indicates. He demonstrates in over 300 pages how the media are biased in favor of conservative viewpoints, big business, and the status quo.

The first few chapters have an identical format — (a) a problem and (b) documented proof of the media's neglect of this crucial problem during the 1960's. The problems he approaches are hunger, auto safety, cigarettes, and cancer, and later in the book VD, prison conditions, and organized crime. These chapters are convincing but hardly exciting to read and are definitely dated.

The heart of the book and its most interesting reading is found in the middle chapters — "Prostitution: A Problem in Definition" (title derived from Theodore Dreiser's comment that "The American press, with very few exceptions is a kept press. Kept by big corporations the way a whore is kept by a rich man."), "How to Become Newsworthy," and "A Catalog of Hidden Bias." Any one of these chapters is well worth the cost of the entire book.

Don't Blame the People is not the kind of book that could be used as a text. Cirino himself has plenty of bias in his research, but any teacher should be able to mine it for a few dozen teaching ideas for a media course.

Exploring Television by William Kuhns (Loyola University Press, 3441 North Ashland Avenue, Chicago, IL 60657) bears a 1971 copyright and was the first "textbook" for a high school class studying commercial television. The 240-page workbook has hundreds of usable suggestions for class activities and discussion, especially on topics such as the various television genres and the images of masculinity, femininity, the family, ethnic groups, and power on the tube.

Although some of the programs mentioned in the book are now part of history, the text's approach is surprisingly undated. At the very least a teacher of a course in television will find *Exploring Television* a rich source of ideas.

Mass Communications and American Empire by Herbert Schiller (Beacon Press, Boston, 1971, 170 pages) is for the serious student of mass media. There are only a few books on "picture tube imperialism" and this still remains the best even though many of the statistics (circa 1966) are dated. Schiller explores the hold of American media on foreign countries. He sees the poor, have-not nations standing "practically defenseless before a rampaging Western commercialism. Impoverished as they are, many developing states are able to afford the new communications complexes only by accepting commercial packages which tie their broadcasting systems to foreign programming and financial sponsorship." Schiller presents a serious and often neglected aspect of global television that should be part of a media teacher's awareness.

The Mind Managers by Herbert Schiller (Beacon Press, Boston, 256 pages) proposes that the consciousness of almost every American is programmed. Most of us have some sense of freedom, some sense of individual choice, a belief in objectivity, and an acceptance of harmony as descriptive of the social condition. What Schiller asks is why and how does the knowledge industry — recreation and entertainment, polling, advertising, publishing, TV and radio — use these beliefs in influencing and creating attitudes and behavior?

On freedom of the press he writes: "Though it cannot be verified, the odds are that the illusion of informational choice is more pervasive in the United States than anywhere else in the world. The illusion is sustained by a confusion, deliberately maintained by the information controllers, that mistakes abundance of media with diversity of content."

About news Schiller says, "When the totality of a social issue is deliberately destroyed and random bits are offered as 'information,' the result is guaranteed: incomprehension at best, ignorance in any case, and apathy and indifference for the most part." He concludes with a provocative analysis of how the government increasingly orchestrates the media and of how the "new technology" is a means of political homogenization.

Schiller has written an important book. It seems likely that those whose minds have been most managed will find the book least acceptable.

Power to Persuade: Mass Media and the News by Robert Cirino (Bantam) should prove a valuable addition to the idea arsenal of any media teacher and could even be used as a text. Relying heavily on news items of the past few years, Cirino documents how the media produce, distribute, and distort major issues of the day. Over 150 fully documented case studies in media decisions are presented. Topics covered include how stories are selected for coverage, how the media sell access to advertisers, sources of news, techniques of non-print media, alternative media systems, censorship, journalistic objectivity, news and advertising, and political viewpoints promoted by entertainment shows.

The bulk of the book consists of twenty-six brief chapters. Each begins with a test case asking the reader what he would do in a particular situation and then reveals what really happened. Next follows a series of "media decisions," usually revealing censorship or distortion of news from recent years, then three or four "activities," often involving role-playing, and finally a few well-chosen questions for discussion. *Power to Persuade* presents more information and thought-provoking activities about the news media *for its price* than any other book I've seen.

TV Action Book by Jeffrey Schrank (McDougal, Littell & Co.,, 1973, 128 pages) is a student "text" about which I can hardly be objective. The book takes a workbook-type approach and can be used for a mini-course or a full-fledged investigation of local television stations. Topics covered by articles and research activities include the fairness doctrine, ownership of local media, news coverage, bias in television, kidvid, violence on television, advertising and counter-advertising, the effect of television on the social environment. The book is a reminder that the airwaves are owned by citizens who have an obligation to demand that they be used to their benefit. The book is very up-to-date, flexible, and nicely inexpensive.

4

Creativity Training: Escaping the Deception That Logic Is All

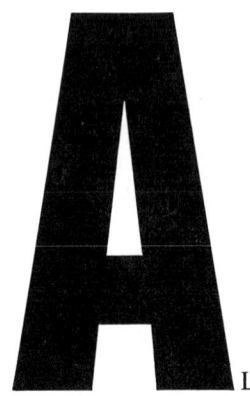

ALBERT EINSTEIN once attributed the creativity of a famous scientist to the fact that he "never went to school, and therefore preserved the rare gift of thinking freely." There is undoubtedly truth in Einstein's observation; many artists and geniuses seem to view their schooling as a hindrance. But such a truth is not a condemnation of schools. It is the function of schools to civilize, not to train explorers. The explorer is inevitably a lonely individual, whether his or her pioneering be in art, music, science, or technology. The creative explorer of unmapped lands shares with the genius what William James described as the "faculty of perceiving in an unhabitual way." Insofar as schools teach perceptual patterns they tend to obliterate creativity and genius. But if schools could somehow exist solely to cultivate genius, then society would degenerate. For the social order demands unity, coherence, and widespread agreement, all traits that are anathema to creativity. There will always be conflict between the demands of society and the impulses of creativity and genius.

Creativity is seen most clearly in those least civilized — children. Infants are, by necessity, totally creative. They have not yet been taught how to handle new situations, so they create their own solutions. Their creativity is not productive of masterpieces nor is it disciplined, but it is truly creative. The similarities between much of modern art and the drawings of children are more than coincidence. Picasso once remarked, "Adults should not teach children to draw, they should learn from them." The child constantly asks why of the world and every experience is a new one, filled with wonder and awe.

Around age five the conflict between the needs of society and the urge to explore exerts itself through required schooling. The children are taught to think logically; they are given answers so that further questions are not needed. For most, the world becomes matter-of-fact and the whys no longer worth asking.

The point of this chapter is not to suggest that schools aim to cultivate genius or even make the most creative student their prime concern. For a good artist is a deadly enemy of society while schools serve as the law and order of the mind and manners. James Agee realized that "No society, no matter how good, could be mature enough to support a real artist without moral danger to that artist. Only no one need worry; for this same good artist is about the one sort of human being who can be trusted to take care of himself." What Agee observed about the artist applies to the highly creative person in any discipline.

The creative urge will exert itself in spite of school and no education reformer will make the classroom a haven for genius. The problem is not one of urging on the genius, but rather one of keeping alive the creativity in each and every student. The deception under which schools seem to function is that logic is the only valid mental process. This distorted emphasis is a roadblock to creative thought.

Because of this concentration on logic, schools have neglected what Jerome Bruner calls right-handed thinking, what Robert Ornstein calls intuition, what Edward De Bono calls lateral thinking, and what many people mean when they say creativity.

Educator-researcher Robert Samples posits the theory that because of this infatuation with logic, schools are developing only one side of the human brain. The analogic/metaphoric/inventive side of the brain is underdeveloped.

ACTIVITIES TO KEEP CREATIVITY ALIVE

The practical teaching ideas which follow are weighted toward "the other side of the brain," toward developing creativity. Ideally they could be part of a course in "Creativity Training." But school curricula are sliced with the logic of subject-matter divisions so that such a course stands little chance of being offered in most schools. For this reason the ideas offered here are written to fit nicely in any kind of creative-writing course.

Most schools currently offer courses in composition and a later course in creative writing. This division seems to suggest that composition is uncreative. I would like to suggest that either of these courses be CREATIVE writing rather than creative WRITING. Each of the activities which follows teaches something about the creative process as well as encouraging students to create and use the intuitive side of the brain.

Imitations

The fact that no two snowflakes are alike is amazing only when we realize this is typical of nature rather than the exception. There are no two trees, flowers, or people alike. It took the human invention of the machine to introduce the reality of manufacturing precise duplicates. A person running a machine can produce duplicates, but a human being alone can make only imitations. In each imitation there will be the stamp of inherent human creativity. What would be an imperfection for a machine is what is most desired in "hand-made" objects. The fact that one cannot make exact duplicates and the fact that each person has creative ability are two ways of stating the same truth.

Any attempt to imitate allows for individual creativity, often unconsciously expressed. Many people cannot be "creative" on command from a teacher, their creativity sneaks out when few are watching. To suggest that "copying" is educational is a bit heretical, but it is also very human. If a teacher believes in the inherent creative ability of each person, imitation as a deadening process need not be feared. Imitation is often the mother of creation.

Poems

In attempting to imitate poems students quickly learn there might be a reason why the words "imitation" and "limitation" are so similar. An attempt to imitate a poem as exactly as possible (number of syllables, stresses, rhyme schemes) imposes a very strict format. The restriction itself forces creative effort in order to remain within its confines.

Select a short poem for the students to imitate. They are to produce a poem that sounds exactly like the original but has a different topic and different words, but words like "a," "the," "of," etc., can be left unchanged. For example, Archibald MacLeish's poem about what a poem should be begins:

A poem should be palpable and mute
As a globed fruit

A student attempting to imitate this poem but assigned to write about either a graveyard or an automobile began:

A graveyard would be wonderful and warm
As a spring storm

Assigning a choice of two or three topics imposes further limitation and produces an amazing variety of approaches. Many of the resulting poems sound surprisingly good and the imitation will produce some genuine insights. The assignment requires careful attention to the sound of words and accents as well as rhymes.

Writing Style

To draw attention to writing style and to engage students in further creative struggle, have them attempt to imitate the writing style of particular authors (ones students have studied during the year would be best) or genres. Students could write a Faulkner or a Hemingway paragraph, an Updike description, or select a more popular "profane" stylist. They could write prose or poetry in imitation of those strictest of all styles — a telegram, the dictionary, a recipe, or a newspaper story. Depending on the ability of the students, the assignment could be simply to capture a particular style any way the student wants or students could be provided with a writing sample for imitation. This latter assignment would be similar to the poetry copying but would not require so exact an imitation.

Connections, Chance, and Playing Around

The most creative writing ever produced by human beings is nothing more than an alphabet in disorder. The by now mythical roomful of monkeys with typewriters and an infinite amount of time could indeed produce *Hamlet*. On their way to producing *Hamlet*, however, they would undoubtedly turn out a few thousand poems, short stories, and paragraphs that would rival the best human writing. For the monkeys, like the best of writers, are only word arrangers.

The difference between a John Updike novel and an unabridged dictionary is arrangement. The elements of both are the same limited number of letter combinations that English speakers have agreed are meaningful. The dictionary is arranged with utter logic and so gives the "reader" no surprises or delights. Updike arranges words in ways never before put together, he plays with the unexpected. The difference between Noah Webster's successors and John Updike is the distance between competence and creativity. There is little room for creative play in arranging a dictionary.

In fact, the creative person can almost be defined as a habitual rearranger and connector, whether of words or ideas, pictures, sounds, devices, or images. This playful arranging might produce something startling, creative, artistic, inventive, humorous, or at least "different." The person who tries only whatever is most logical misses the chance for a serendipitous discovery.

An uncreative cook, for example, might be very competent as a meal provider, even able to produce feasts for a gourmet. But the uncreative cook does little more than follow directions in cookbooks. The results will be totally predictable, barring human and mechanical error. The creative cook, by contrast, might also follow recipes but will sometimes try a little culinary experimentation. While deep frying onion rings the creative impulse might strike and the cook will begin to wonder what would happen if an olive were deep fried. By the way, the creative cook will have a higher rate of failure than the merely competent cook but will also enjoy the surprises and delights of chance and experimentation.

Profiles of the creative personality reveal a frequent tendency to "play around with ideas" and hit upon final combinations by chance. The value of chance combinations is not limited to rare instances. Examples of great inventions that have been perfected through accidental discoveries run into the hundreds. The importance of chance lies in the fact that it circumvents the limitations of logic and predictability.

The following exercises encourage serendipity — the chance discovery.

Creativity Training

These exercises attempt to replace logic with play and to teach that a playful spirit is an important part of creativity.

Playing Around #1: New Foods

For this demonstration of the value of chance arrangement and playing around, students are placed in the role of director of ideas for a large food company. Their task is to invent new items for the company to sell in supermarkets. As chief food inventor each person knows that there are only so many foods available, and new vegetables or edible animals are unlikely to turn up on the doorstep. So to invent new foods try crossing old foods with a variety of packaging and processing ideas to create a new product.

Write two lists of words like the following on the blackboard (expand the list if possible):

Packaging	*Foods*
Aerosol can	peanut butter
liquid	pizza
frozen	ice cream
instant	banana splits
dried	soups
gourmet	toothpaste
canned	spinach
squeeze tube	soap

My idea for a new supermarket sensation is:

My name for this new product is:

Playing Around #2: Book Titles

The creative manipulator of words has the power to shape ideas and influence the actions of others. Since words are cheap and common, the creative use of words involves putting them together in new and startling ways. Take the two lists of words below and randomly juxtapose one from each list.

human	children
earth	tornadoes
prefabricated	skyscrapers
instant	doughnuts
scented	hamburgers
lighter than air	shoes
frozen	
mechanical	
disposable	

Out of the matched pair of words from the previous page create a book title:

___

Now add a subtitle to explain the contents:

___

___

Write a 25-word description of the book:

Playing Around #3: Pop Poetry

The first activity rearranged concepts, the second words, and this activity suggests playing around with word environments.

Pop artists often take the ordinary, traditionally non-artistic stuff and junk of everyday life and place it in traditionally artistic locations — in frames or museums. By so doing they encourage people to "see" these ordinary objects perhaps for the first time.

The same environmental rearranging can be done with words to give the ultra-ordinary new meaning. Pop poetry uses the ordinary written instructions and reminders that are so much a part of the environment as to be indivisible. These prosaic messages are arranged in a poetic form or in some creative way to give them new meaning.

Present students some examples of pop poetry. A few are given below (A collection of poetry-of-the-ordinary is *Pop Poems* by Ronald Gross. The book is in paperback from Simon & Schuster and was originally published in 1967.)

THANK YOU – COME AGAIN

Close cover before striking.
   Thank you—come again.
Please pay cashier.
   Thank you—come again.
We appreciate your patronage.
   Thank you—come again.
Service is our middle name.
   Thank you—come again.
Another satisfied customer.
   Thank you—come again.
The pleasure was ours.
   Thank you—come again.
Here's your correct change.
   Thank you—come again.
We aim to please.
   Thank you—come again.
Thank you—come again.
   Thank you—come again.
Thank you—come again.
   Thank you—come again.

EPIGRAMS

I

The future belongs to the fit.
When this circuit learns your job
   what are you going to do?

II

Vote—for the candidate of your choice.
Every litter bit hurts.

III

The Iron Curtain isn't soundproof.
Give to the college of your choice.

IV

> Put a tiger in your tank.
> Drive Safely.

V

> Why not put *your* message in this space?
> Why not put *your* message in this space?

Playing Around #4: Questions and Answers

Each student should have six index cards or small pieces of paper. On three of the cards write a question of some sort. Make at least one of the questions "philosophical" in nature. (There is no need to explain what philosophical means for this exercise.) On the remaining three cards write three answers that may or may not be replies to the three questions written.

Collect all the questions and all the answers so there is a question pile and an answer pile. Then have a student select a question card at random and read it. Have another student select an answer card at random and read it. Do this just for fun, looking for answers that in some creative way shed new light on the questions. A writing assignment could be given using one of the random matchings as the base.

Playing Around #5: Plots

To aid the creative process of finding writing topics and to illustrate the value of serendipity, create a story or film description by chance.

Write four headings on the blackboard: Characters, Locations, Goals, and Obstacles. Brainstorm among students each column at a time for ideas. A partial list might look like this:

CHARACTERS	LOCATIONS
President of the United States	School
Me	Fred's (local store)
Alice Cooper	Death Valley
Santa Claus	North Pole
God	Mars
A robot	Golf course

Creativity Training

The milkman	Tree house
The principal	Underwater
The Six Million Dollar Man	Airplane
GOALS	**OBSTACLES**
To discover a cure for cancer	A towering inferno
To get married	An earthquake
To gain independence	A wicked stepmother
To survive	An army of three million
Take over the world	mosquitoes
Win a beauty contest	Everyone is afraid
Become famous	An invisible shield
To command the first Mars shot	A giant magnet
	Starvation

Using the list above have students orally combine various elements to produce synopses of yet to be written stories or films. For example, using the above list one could propose a story about:

> A robot enters Central Catholic High School in order to win a beauty contest but finds himself victimized by a giant magnet in the boys' washroom.
>
> Alice Cooper goes golfing in an attempt to gain worldwide fame as an athlete. One day an army of three million mosquitoes attacks Alice and delivers a stinging blow to his athletic dreams.

Have students write short film descriptions aping the style of *TV Guide* or newspaper plot summaries for films.

Wordplay — Visual and Audio

Poetry can almost be defined (certainly described) as a disciplined playing with words. In the exercise with poem imitation strict limitations were placed on the plan. The following exercises encourage a more free-form play using words both as a printed image and as sounds.

Visual Wordplay

The simplest starting point for playing with words is to have students try writing words in such a way that their appearance is itself meaningful. The best examples I've found of this kind of creativity are in Robert Carola's occasional "Word Play" page in *Playboy*. Examples of "shaped words" include:

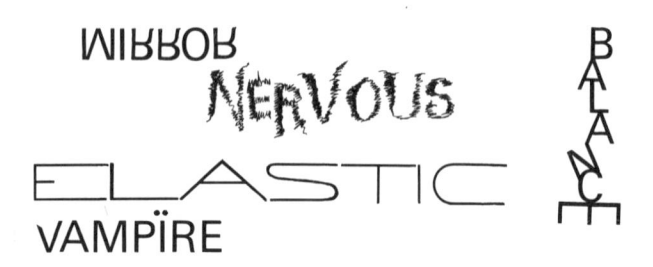

MIRROR (mirrored)   NERVOUS (shaky)   BATANCY (vertical, stacked)

ELASTIC (stretched)   VAMPĪRE

Have students create and collect meaningfully shaped words. Fill blackboards and bulletin boards with them.

From these simple, single words students can move on to poetry written in a shape that lends the poem additional meaning. The best examples of this integration of a poem's appearance and its meaning are e.e. cummings' poems "1(a" and "one" and "un." Brief explanations of these poems along with ideas for using them in the classroom can be found in David Burmester's fine article, "Poems on the Wall" in the November 1968 issue of *Media & Methods* magazine.

From e.e. cummings the leap to concrete poetry is more like a small step. Concrete poems play with words both as black shapes on white space and as abstract conveyors of meaning. For example, the word/building on the next page uses only one word to make a very clear statement.

Show students examples of concrete poems (an overhead projector will help) and then have them write their own poems working alone and/or in groups. A number of collections of concrete poems have been published. The best book for student use is a small paperback from Xerox Educational Publications, *Concrete is Not Always Hard,* edited by Barbara Pilon.

More literary collections are *An Anthology of Concrete Poetry* edited by Emmett Williams and published in 1967 by Something Else Press, P.O. Box H, Barton, VT 05822; also Eve Merriam's *Finding a Poem* published in 1970 by Atheneum Publishers. Another collection of concrete

Creativity Training   111

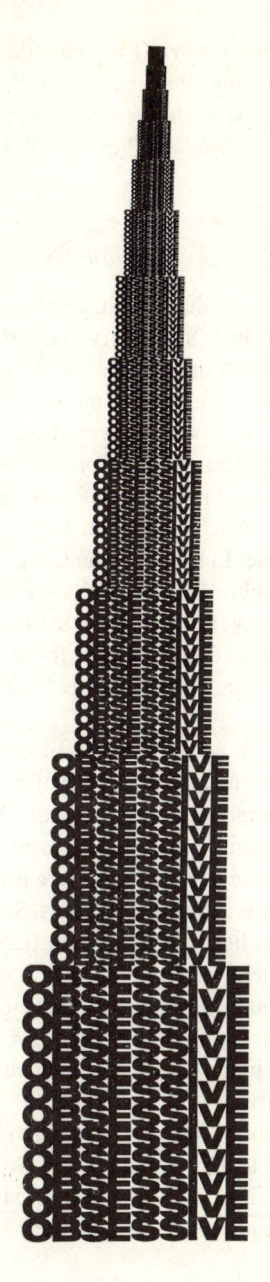

—Gay Reineck

poems is *Concrete Poetry: A World View* edited by Mary Ellen Solt and published in 1970 by Indiana University Press, Bloomington, IN 47401. Another useful collection is *Anthology of Concretism* edited by Eugene Wildman and published by Swallow Press, 1139 S. Wabash Ave., Chicago, IL 60605.

Audio Wordplay

Concrete poetry recognizes that the shape of the word is important and is thus firmly established as a literary art. But words also have sounds, even though a sound once made is lost forever while a letter lives as long as the material it is written on holds together. Poetry was originally an oral art and only since universal literacy and the perfection of inexpensive printing processes has its oral element taken second place to its letter/appearance. Oral poetry is nearly a lost art. The most common examples of poems which depend on sound are Carl Sandburg's "Cool Tombs" and Vachel Lindsay's "The Congo." Both are readily available on records in public libraries and serve as a nice introduction to the oral aspect of poetry. Give the students the poem first in print. After having them read it and talk about it for at least a few minutes present the recorded version to demonstrate how the sound of a poem can make it come alive.

After this introduction move on to a few selections from the records of *Poetry-Out-Loud* — a triannual stereo LP of poems that defy printing. The poems on these records *are* the sounds, the performance, the effect of sound on emotions — there are no printed versions of the poems. *Poetry-Out-Loud* recognizes that there is no longer a need to destroy or confine a poem in a prison of print. Sheet music and printed scores have never been confused with the reality of music, but printed poems have somehow become the norm of poetry, an art which was originally a purely audio experience. *Poetry-Out-Loud* represents the most creative current discovery of poetry for the ear, an exploration of the limits of the human voice and an adventure on the thin line between speech and music.

Each album contains about thirteen poems that range in mood from meditative and mystical to earthy and sensual. Some sound like *a capella* rock, others are filled with moans and wailings echoed and re-echoed. The poems often depend on multi-track tape effects, delays, and reverberation to achieve an eerie and enveloping mood. (For current price information write *Poetry-Out-Loud*, 39 Ridgetop Drive, St. Louis, MO 63117.)

Since most students have access to tape recorders (or sound equipment used for music), they can create their own oral poetry.

A less "poetic" but equally oral wordplay is Ken Nordine's "Word Jazz." In a series of Dot records made in the 1960's Nordine free-associated around a theme backed by jazz musicians. Nordine describes the word jazz as a "thought followed by a thought followed by a thought *ad infinitum* – a kind of wonder-wandering. . . . Imagine the imagination as a jazz instrument wailing words, verbal riffs that swing from images to ideas to images, a kind of oscillating curiosity creating far-in far-out fantasies on some fact . . . ."

The word jazz albums are now out of print but can be found in cut-out bins and dusty "Spoken Word" sections of large record stores or in libraries. The most useful word jazz album is probably the *Classic Collection: The Best of Word Jazz, Ken Nordine Volume Three* on Dot DLP 25880. The album contains the "Bury-it-Yourself Time Capsule" which suggests that if buildings can have time capsules why not everyman? "Adult Kindergarten" is another of the album's more fascinating cuts suggesting that all adults would benefit greatly from a second kindergarten.

Both *Poetry-Out-Loud* and word jazz can help students who find the printed word an obstacle to expression.

Creative Interpretation: The Search for Alternatives

It is characteristic of creative people to seek out alternatives. Those who habitually seek alternatives are much more likely to hit upon creative solutions to problems. The very process of seeking an alternative is creative while the habit of consistently choosing the familiar is in itself limiting.

The following exercises are intended to encourage the habit of seeking alternatives. These exercises will not develop the alternatives *habit*, but they will provide insight into the process of seeking alternatives so that students can practice on their own to make generating a variety of options a familiar process.

1. Photo Interpretation

Using slides or large pictures from magazines or newspapers, ask students to describe what they see. After a few answers ask them to list as many alternative interpretations as possible.

For example, a photo of children playing around an open fire hydrant on a hot day produced descriptive labels of:

Children playing by a fire hydrant
Kids cooling off in the street
Kids splashing around a fire hydrant
Some kids who opened a hydrant playing
  before the cops stop them

A few more descriptive labels were supplied for the photo and then students were asked what else the picture could possibly be. Students were asked for answers that are very unlikely yet still describe the picture. Some of their replies included:

Kids trying to flood the street so cars couldn't get through so they could play ball on the street
A broken hydrant that some Cub Scouts are trying to fix by sitting on it. They're taking turns sitting on it.
Lake Michigan oozing up through the street
A spaceman from another planet who shoots water through his head playing with some kids he thinks are adults.
A crew of city workmen in a time when children have taken over the world. They're trying to fix the broken hydrant and enjoying their work.

Pictures presented for creative interpretation can be as straightforward as the one described above or more obscure and abstract like those frequently found in photography magazines. You can also use an inkblot — the most obvious interpretations are often given first and then more creative alternatives are explored.

No attempt should be made to judge the interpretations right or wrong nor should any be labeled as "the most creative." The point of this exercise is to encourage the process of seeking alternative interpretations.

2. Scoring

Mention scoring to a class of students above fifth grade and they will immediately reveal if they are more interested in sports or the opposite sex. But scoring has another meaning useful as an aid in developing creative habits. A score is a series of annotations that give directions, such as a musical score. In traditional musical scoring, each interpreter will produce quite similar results depending on the level of skill and nuances. Some experimenters in "new music" have played with the idea that traditional scoring does not allow enough room for creative expression. And so they have sought more ambiguous scores such that no performer will even remotely repeat another's performances.

One such musical score titled "Serenade II Janice Wentworth" by Ted Greer and Charles Amirkhanian appears below:

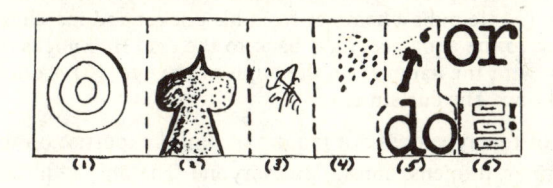

The score for "Serenade II Janice Wentworth" is a collection of performance stimuli rather than a strict set of directions. Amirkhanian explains how his composition can be performed.

> There is no single way to perform any one of my scores. Each one of them is simply a matrix containing performance stimuli. What we are dealing with, then, is a finished drawing – in itself a "work of art" – which in turn will serve as the stimulus for another work of art, i.e., a performance of music or a play, the making of a painting or a sculpture, the presentation of a series of events, ad infinitum – or preferably, any combination of the foregoing. Contained in each matrix are various visual images. It is from these images that the artist will derive the individual actions which will constitute a performance.
> The composer has developed various major areas in the score. Within each area is a series of images which is intended to evoke responses. The six images shown could affect various artists, for example, in the following ways:
> A. As played by a concert musician, specifically a percussionist.
> (1) strikes gong; (2) plays record of music from Russian Orthodox Mass on portable phonograph; (3) scratches butt end of xylophone in

middle and high registers; (5) utters the word "due" while raising hammer, and "doe" while smashing a walnut; (6) utters "or . . ." and proceeds to exit by means of the nearest visible door.

B. As performed by a painter as a performance piece, or a finished product, or both. (1) throws ten darts at the blank canvas, puncturing it; (2) squeezes a full tube of white paint onto the surface of the canvas; (3) brushes on ink delicately; (4) paints several of the dart holes a bright red; (5) paints an apple on the canvas — there is a large nail in the apple — the apple is bleeding; (6) wires an oar to the canvas — under the oar is painted the word "door."

C. As realized by a theatrical director, dramatist, or actor. (1) The curtain rises; onstage is an enormous plastic eyeball, fifteen feet in diameter, staring straight ahead. (2) A man walks onstage in front of the eye, stops, spreads his legs, raises his hands above his head, and places his palms together. (3) Fifteen seconds later he lowers his arms and shuffles his feet as if attempting to tap dance. (4) He stomps his right foot repeatedly and at various volume levels in mock frustration. (5) He pulls a hammer from his pocket and marches, with his back to the audience, right back to the eye. He knocks once very sharply with the hammer on the pupil of the eye. (6) A door slams behind him. The curtain falls.

A score of this type does not require technical expertise on the part of the performer, it opens "music" to everyone. The only requirement is a willingness to seek creative interpretations.

Present this score to students along with the explanations of how others performed it. Ask for other possible interpretations. Finally, ask students to prepare their own "new music scores." The score does not have to be a series of six sketches; any images that can be taken as a "collection of performance stimuli" will do.

Allow time for the construction of the scores and then bring them all to class, swap them and have a performance day. The performances are more interesting if a variety of props are available. One way to provide them is to swap scores a few days before performance day and have each student prepare one interpretation of one score and bring the needed props. All the props are then made available (in a pile) for spontaneous and alternative performances.

3. Problem Solving

Use the same kind of generation of alternatives applied to the photos and scores to solve some practical problem. You could practice with a

Creativity Training

problem from the newspaper or an advice column. Be sure to end this section on the habit of searching for alternatives by trying to solve some practical class or school problem.

Meditation on a Bunch of Grapes

Some producers of educational media have introduced filmstrip or slide units that claim to "awaken the senses of students" so they can write better. Certainly there is truth in the realization that a heightened sense of awareness improves the quality of descriptive writing. But to show two-dimensional, untouchable, odorless, Kodachrome images to awaken senses would seem a last resort fitting only for a prolonged interstellar space voyage. Such visual stimuli have value but should not be allowed to replace reality.

One exercise which often produces writing more creative than usual from students is a meditation on a bunch of grapes. The exercise begins by giving each student a small bunch of grapes (two to four grapes per bunch will suffice — largesse depends on the departmental budget for fruit) to be examined carefully, "as if you've never seen a grape before in your life." An observation sheet can be given to each student. Such a sheet would look something like the following:

Do the following with your grapes (jotting down notes after each step might prove helpful):
1. Examine them visually very carefully — pull one off the stem.
2. Peel one grape. Smell the grape.
3. Hold the peeled grape up to the brightest light available and look through it.
4. Squash a grape with your fingers.
5. Eat the peeled grape. Eat an unpeeled grape.
6. If there are seeds, examine them visually and taste one.

After completing the above examination write creative answers to the following requests for information and analogies:
1. Select the most perfect grape in your bunch. Describe its perfection as a thing of wondrous beauty.
2. Describe a grape to someone who has never seen one.
3. A grape is to a bunch of grapes as a _____ is to a _____.
4. A peeled grape held up to the light is like a _____.

5. List one or two things you discovered about grapes you never knew before.

6. Peeling a grape is like _____.

7. The smell of a grape is _____.

8. My favorite recreational activity is squashing grapes because it's like _____.

9. The taste of a grape is to canned grape juce as _____.

10. I am like a grape in that _____.

11. What is the sound of a grape?

Discuss the various answers with the class. If the answers are not particularly creative, try some group brainstorming to improve them. Ask if anyone learned anything about creative writing from the grape meditations. My own experience is that the general level of writing is more creative than with a normal assignment.

The point of this exercise is to demonstrate the value of something real to write about and use as a basis for metaphors and comparison. The exercise also points out that even familiar objects have secrets to be revealed upon close observation. A follow-up assignment could be given to write one creative sentence (or paragraph, poem, story) using the grape as a central image or character.

Storming Brains

Brainstorming as a problem-solving technique was first described in print by advertising executive Alex Osborn. His book, *Applied Imagination*, now in its thirty-second printing since publication in 1953, is described in "Resource Paperbacks" at the end of this chapter.

Brainstorming is more than a meeting of people tossing around ideas. It is a technique with a definite structure and rules that must be followed in order to be effective and it must deal with a *very* specific problem. Because brainstorming is such an effective way to stimulate creativity everyone should experience its power at some time.

In a brainstorming session there are four basic rules.

1. No ideas may be criticized or put down — there is no evaluation during the idea-gathering period.

2. Ideas do not have to be practical. The wilder the idea the better. Wacky, unrealistic, idealistic, and just plain silly ideas are welcome.

3. Strive for quantity. The more ideas the better.

4. Combine. Brainstormers could combine ideas already mentioned by others or improve ideas already given.

Another very important part of the brainstorming technique is to deal with a specific problem. A problem stated in general terms such as "how can we improve schools?" is not as good as "How can we improve this school?" But neither idea is as effective as "How can we get students to keep the cafeteria clean?" A brainstorming session that never develops more than a drizzle of ideas is very likely plagued by a problem stated too generally or vaguely.

One person should be designated as an idea collector to write ideas on a blackboard or paper. The blackboard is preferred since it helps to see other ideas.

A brainstorming session should last only as long as ideas are forthcoming from the participants. After all the ideas are written down, discussion about their practicality and implementation can begin. It is very important that such discussion not take place during the brainstorming session itself.

To demonstrate brainstorming to a class, select a creative topic that is simple, a bit wacky, and without relevance. A few good examples include:

You have just inherited 100,000 old 78 rpm phonograph records that no one else wants. (They have no monetary value.) How could you possibly dispose of the records profitably?

How many uses for a paper clip other than clipping paper together can you list?

What sort of device would you invent to enable people to walk on water?

How can you improve a vacuum cleaner so that millions more people will buy one?

How could you package an egg so that it could be dropped from the school roof to the ground without breaking?

After establishing the format of a brainstorm session and experiencing it, move on to some practical problem. Define the problem very specifically before you begin.

If an assignment is desired, you might suggest that students conduct a brainstorm session to solve a problem in some other group (a school extracurricular activity, a work situation, at home, etc.) sometime within the next month.

A brainstorming session can be used as a creative writing stimulus. Robert Samples, in the February 1975 issue of *Learning* magazine describes a free-association exercise that is a variation on brainstorming. Begin by writing some word on the blackboard (he uses "gravity" as an example); then ask students to free-associate words or short phrases. Do not rephrase anything the students call out — write all ideas on the blackboard.

According to Samples, most of the early ideas will be of a quite logical (and probably uncreative) nature. When the student response slows to a near stop, suggest that students now switch to the funniest, wackiest, weirdest things they can think of that relate to the word. This will spark a flood of new responses. When the silly ideas slow to a dribble, ask students to invent new words by combining words and phrases already on the board.

Then have them write a poem, paragraph, introduction to a story, poem or story fragment, anything using the ideas from the free-association brainstorming session. The purpose of the assignment is to stimulate and actually bring to life the creative impulse, so the resulting writing should not be judged for grammar or "correctness."

A sample from one such "wordstorming" session follows:

SURVIVE	SURVIVAL
(phase one words)	(phase three words)
Live	Robinson Apeman
Cope	Cannibal's Island
Get along	1000-year-old ice cream
Die	Survival of the oldest
Island	Ice cream island
Wilderness	Breathing hunter
Breathing	The last ape on earth
Poison	Reincarnation defense
Hold on life	Reincaruso
Age	Escape the grave
This side of grave	Atomic ice cream
Escape	Shelter island
Outlive	Eat hunters

Fittest
Grow old
Evolution
Eat
How to . . .
Last person on earth

(phase two words)
Ice cream pie
Robinson Caruso
Space suit
2001
Hunter
Hunted
Jungle
Indians
Cannibals
Atomic Bomb
Peace
Shelter
Air Raid Siren
Civil Defense
Thousand-Year-Old Man
Reincarnation
No death
Planet of the Apes

Space suit wilderness
Space cannibals
Robinson Caruso in 2001
1000-Year-Old Indian

Using the above as creative stumulus one student wrote the opening paragraph to a science fiction novel:

Robinson Apeman was a cannibal. But now that no one was left how could he eat? Alone on an island of atomic ice cream ash, floating in a sea of poisoned waters, he was the last man on earth. It had been 1,000 years since the war and the peace of death had been denied only him. His space suit had saved him but had now become his personal wilderness and future tomb.

Imagination Projection

A creative person is able to assume a variety of viewpoints and see numerous potential solutions to problems. Part of this ability to transcend a single limited viewpoint comes from the willingness to enter into the mind-set of another person or to identify with an object or situation. The creative person projects her- or himself into different worlds of the imagination.

This creative journey of the imagination is particularly useful to those in the dramatic arts who can use projection to actually become the character they are asked to play on stage or screen. But imagination projection can also help any kind of creative expression from writing to painting or even the creative solution of practical problems.

Imagination projection is nothing more than the childhood art of "pretending," of creating inhabitable worlds of "make-believe." This childhood pastime is the foundation of fiction, drama, film, and sometimes art. As is so often the case in creativity enhancement, the following exercises require a recovery of the inherent imagination of youth coupled with the wisdom of experience.

Projection Exercise #1: Imagine You Are . . .

An assignment that will help limber up the ligaments of the imagination asks students to write a short piece from the viewpoint of another person or thing. In this assignment the students are to try to imagine themselves as being a specific person or thing. The writing would therefore be in the first person; it should not be *about* the subject, it should be the subject writing.

Some ideas that have produced creative results include:

Imagine you are a rat who yearns for the good old days before plastic garbage cans.

Imagine you are suddenly transported to a strange island where everyone is blind. You are the only person with sight.

Imagine you are a baby being born.

Imagine yourself as a television set forced to look at people most of the day.

Write a diary entry for August 14, 2001 — you are the last person on earth.

You are a snowflake, unique and different from all other snowflakes, yet no one recognizes you in the snowfall.

Projection Exercise #2: The Astral Anthropologist

This exercise is simply a variant of the "Imagine You Are . . ." writing assignment. In this imagination stretcher students assume the role of an anthropologist from outer space who comes to earth and files a report on the state of the earth to his home planet. This anthropologist must base his or her report only on observations wherever he or she (or it) lands. The report should be in writing.

In order to stimulate ideas present students a few examples of the creative work of others along this same line. One of the best appeared in *American Anthropologist* of June 1956. The article is "Body Ritual Among the Nacirema" by Horace Miner and details an anthropologist's view of Americans' obsession with cleanliness and bathrooms. The satire was reprinted in *Everyman His Way*, edited by Alan Deindes, published by Prentice-Hall in 1966 as a student textbook.

In Pierre Berton's *My War With the 20th Century* (Doubleday, 1966) there is a section in which an archeological expedition to the former site of New York uncovers various relics that need interpretation. Parking meters are labeled shrines to roadside gods, and barbeque grills are identified as places of animal sacrifice.

Robert Nathan's small and very hard-to-find book *The Weans* (Knopf, 1956) is another fantasy of a future excavation of the United States.

The most accessible report to another planet on "earthlings" is a short film produced by the National Film Board of Canada called *What on Earth?* This animated film takes the form of a report from Martian observers on a new planet — earth. The Martians understandably think that autos are the real inhabitants of earth. With this mistaken assumption the logical consequences are not only hilarious but also thought-provoking. Road signs are thought to be the means of earthling's education, food is gas and oil, garages are medical centers, and the ultimate purpose of individuals is to be sent to a "retirement park" (junkyard), there to reproduce. What do the Martians think of people? Parasites of course, pesky little things that the autos seem well on their way towards eliminating. (The 10-minute animated film is available for sale or rental from Contemporary/McGraw-Hill Films, 828 Custer Avenue, Evanston, IL 60202 or offices in New York or San Francisco.)

Before students write from the viewpoint of an astral anthropologist, ideas can be stimulated by an exchange of ideas with a fellow explorer. Have students pair off and role-play the situation of two explorers from some other planet who have landed on earth in different places and now meet for the first time to compare notes. To guide the conversation, suggest students compare notes on things they saw that surprised them, that frightened them, that confused them. Do the earthlings seem friendly? Are they an advanced or backward civilization?

Projection Exercise #3: You Are That

Imaginative projection is not limited to the artistic process, childhood, or courses in creative writing. Everyone projects constantly, most often on subconscious level. Unconscious projection, the tendency to identify oneself with the world "out there," is what makes objectivity impossible. We see things not as *they* are but as *we* are. Therefore, there is no such thing as objectivity, only varying degrees of subjectivity. Because everyone projects a bit of the self into the world out there, reactions to a painting, a book, a film, or even a piece of furniture vary considerably.

An extreme example of unconscious projection is the experiencing of one's own feelings, mood, or attitude as belonging instead to someone or something "out there." A violent person will often disown his own violent tendencies and project them onto what he will see as a violent, cruel world. Carried too far, this projection results in a person's being unable to accept his own feelings.

That unconscious projection is a constant process can be illustrated in an exercise that both stretches the imagination and could lead to a bit of self-knowledge.

Instruct each person in the room to look around and focus on a specific object that attracts the attention. The object must be visible and specific — that piece of chalk sitting on the ledge rather than chalk in general. Once all have selected an object, instruct them to identify with the object, become the object; "As the object, describe how you feel, why you are there, what you are doing. Do not talk about 'it,' always use 'I.' " This should be done quietly with each person writing down some of the observations on paper that will not be collected. A person might say to himself, if the piece of chalk is the object chosen, "I am white and smooth and help people to say what they want. Every time someone uses me I get a little smaller until some day I will be only dust."

After a few minutes of silent monologue toss out a few ideas that will help those who are stalled and have "nothing more to say." Remind students to describe themselves (as the object) in relation to other things in the room, ask how they feel about being a _____. "What could be done to improve you? what don't you like about being here? what do you like about being here? what purpose do you serve?"

Allow more time for interior monologues and the writing of observations. Stress that the writing should be for reference only and that this is not an assignment in creative writing.

When all are finished, have them reconsider everything they said and wrote about the object but this time applying the statements to themselves. See how many of the statements while projecting were really true statements about the self. Students are often amazed at how accurately they have described themselves, even in regard to personality traits they prefer not to admit.

This technique is sometimes used in encounter groups solely for its value in self-revelation. John Enright, the popularizer of the technique, tells of a woman who identified with a beam in the ceiling and said to herself, "I'm very old-fashioned and uselessly ornate. . . . I have a heavy load to bear . . . and I'm not getting very much help; the nearest other beam is a long way away, and I have to carry this part of the load alone." The woman realized through the exercise that this was a description of herself, a self-concept she had been hiding from herself for years.

This "You Are That" exercise described here is not intended for use in analyzing students' motivations, but if it helps students understand themselves a bit, so much the better. It is intended to point out that projection is a constant process that can be utilized for creative purposes.

Cliché Consciousness

High school and college students are by now quite accustomed to receiving writing assignments back from teachers with the word "cliché" written in red near a circled phrase. The teacher sees such a correction as a helpful observation and a warning to "sin no more." To the student, however, such labeling is often merely a sign of the pet peeves of an arbitrary teacher.

That clichés are undesirable has become itself a kind of cliché, a rule often invoked but seldom examined. Clichés are worth avoiding in writing for two reasons, one having to do with cybernetics and one with creativity. Anyone with even a slight knowledge of information theory knows the general rule of communication which states, "The more probable the message, the less information it gives." A cliché, being of high probability, communicates little, precisely because it is so expected. The cliché is easily incorporated into already held ideas and beliefs and so is quite incapable of penetrating the mind of the receiver to communicate something new or challenging.

The second reason that clichés are worth avoiding is that they encourage the mind to work along already well-worn paths. They are civilizing factors that discourage exploration of new ways of expression. The cliché is a convenient way to avoid the effort needed to be creative.

Having thus branded clichés as factors which encourage stagnation of creativity, the problem remains to recognize a cliché before a wrting teacher labels it as such. Part of the reason students use clichés so much is that they don't know phrases are clichés. One person's cliché is another's bright new discovery of the week. Cliché recognition requires experience in reading and writing. But to help speed up this experience there is a classroom exercise that does help students become aware of clichés.

After a brief discussion of clichés brainstorm with the class for a blackboard full of clichés. Perhaps have each student find a number of clichés in writing or have each student write a paragraph using only clichés.

Find and bring to class a dictionary of clichés and read some to the class. For each cliché have the class write a creative way of communicating the idea expressed by the cliché. The alternatives need not be suitable for framing, they need by only original and appropriate. Some of the results might look like this:

CLICHÉ	ALTERNATIVES
(use the cliché in a sentence)	
. . . as a fish takes to water	. . . as a baby takes to crying
	. . . as a flower takes to sunlight
	. . . as flies cluster by garbage cans
. . . racked her brains	Ideas sizzled in her head like bacon on a griddle.
	. . . searched her mind with the desperation of a prisoner seeking escape from the gas chamber
	Her mind raced like a field of four-minute racers.
. . . passed the buck	. . . shared problems with the generosity of Santa Claus
	. . . attacked problems with all the ferocity of a lame turtle.

After this concentrated exposure to clichés students begin to develop a "nose" for the clichéd style of writing. But there still remains one kind of "cliché" never mentioned in writing courses — the personal cliché. A personal cliché is some expression or phrase that a person uses constantly either in speech, writing, or both. A person is usually not aware that he or she overuses a certain phrase, but friends (and enemies) can be quite helpful in pointing out personal clichés.

A class discussion on current speech clichés can lead students to speak more creatively (when they desire) instead of using the current clichés. Students should be aware that often the use of clichés in speech is intentional, designed to share identification with a certain group or lifestyle. Class discussion usually centers in phrases like "you know" or slang expressions. A follow-up assignment is to encourage each student to resolve to avoid a certain personal cliché in speech and to find other, more creative ways to say the same thing.

There is yet another kind of writing that belongs to the cliché family. Certain words are overused by students and often become a top-of-the-head substitute for creative thought. The champion overused word is either "think" or "it."

Select the words that the class tends to overuse and place them on a "dirty word" list. The use of these words then becomes forbidden in writing. The point of the "dirty word" list, it should be clear to students, is not that these words should never be used; the point is that by completely forbidding their use for a given period students are forced to seek alternatives which are invariably better and more creative and they break the habit of using the hackneyed words.

RESOURCE PAPERBACKS FOR A
UNIT IN CREATIVITY

Two books by Edward de Bono: New Think (Avon) and *Lateral Thinking* (Harper Colophon) detail a systematic approach to creative problem-solving. De Bono calls logic "vertical thinking" and claims that creativity demands a different kind of thinking he describes as "lateral thinking." Lateral thinking is an approach to problem-solving that encourages exploration, the consideration of alternatives, the creation of analogies, thought-pattern variations, assumption-challenging, and about a dozen other mental aids.

New Think spends much time talking about the notion of lateral thinking. *Lateral Thinking,* on the other hand, is a very practical how-to description of creative problem-solving. The latter book is highly recommended as a teacher resource for units or a course in creativity.

Strange and Familiar and *Teaching is Learning to Listen* are two small workbooks that give practical exercises in creative analogies. The workbooks are based on W. J. J. Gordon's "synectics" approach to creativity. The system is built on the idea that most situations requiring innovation can be helped by a process of making the familiar strange. Familiarity breeds blocked minds while strangeness demands creativity.

The two paperback workbooks are part of a series of books on synectics available from Synectics Education Systems, 121 Brattle Street, Cambridge, MA 02138.

Applied Imagination by Alex F. Osborn (Scribner's) was written in 1953 and has become a classic for those conducting courses in creative problem-solving. Osborn is the father of brainstorming which he describes in detail in *Applied Imagination.* He also gives other creative techniques and examines factors which block the creative process. The book is practical and oriented toward the creative solution of real-life problems. The bibliography is hopelessly dated, but the ideas are useful.

Your Key to Creative Thinking by Samm Sinclair Baker (Bantam) is the least scientific of the books on this list. Unlike "Lateral Thinking" and "Synectics" which are carefully developed systems, the ideas proposed by Baker are a potpourri of advice and mental tricks. Many of the ideas and much of the advice in Baker's book are useful, but the book is more a self-improvement course than an investigation of creativity. *Your Key to Creative Thinking* contains enough useful ideas and is inexpensive enough to make it a candidate for a student text. It cannot stand on its own as a text and should be used in connection with ideas from the other books on this list.

5

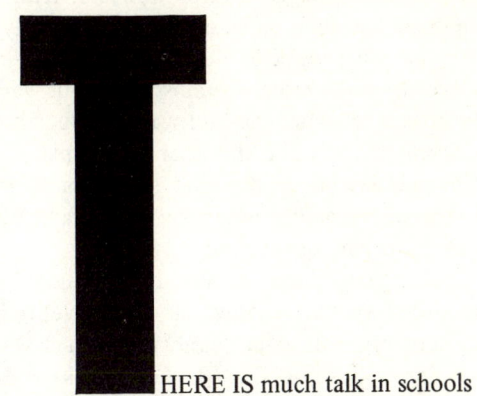

Visual Awareness

THERE IS much talk in schools these days of a "return to the basics." But when asked exactly what these basics are the inevitable reply suggests they are those things taught in schools in the pre-Sputnik days. "Basics" has become a code word for a desire to return to the uncomplicated; nostalgia pure and simple.

But there are truly basic skills that schools have neglected. Skills, in fact, far more basic than the traditional three R's. One of these skills is visual perception. True, a minority of students in high school do receive some art training or film study but the majority are never taught the possibilities of an awakened eye.

Behind the failure to teach a sharpened sense of visual awareness is the deception that SEEING does not have to be taught except to the partially blind. Because we have incorrectly thought that seeing is automatic instead of a skill to be learned, we are in danger of accepting blindness as normal. A child's wide-eyed curiosity at the ever new world is to be envied, for that child will grow up to learn that there is very little worth seeing. He or she will learn that it is acceptable to look at attractive examples of the opposite sex, at pictures with frames hung in museums, at anything that costs $2.50 for admission, and anything labeled "scenic," but not much more.

We do a lot of looking. We look through lenses, at screens and glassed tubes; in fact we look about twelve hours a day, but we see less and less.

We become onlookers, spectators, "subjects" looking at "objects." Quickly we place labels on all that is, labels that stick once and for all. School is a twelve- to twenty-year process of learning which labels go where. By these labels we recognize and identify much but SEE little. We know the labels on all the bottles but rarely taste the wine.

Schools have neglected the art of SEEING. What good is the knowledge of how to put together the most wondrous words if one is blind to what they describe? What good is learning about filmmaking if the eye behind the camera does not SEE? What value is painting to the blindfolded eye? If there is any one quality that is common to artists in all the media, it is this unusual ability to see. An artist is a SEER, a prophet, a one-eyed man in the land of the blind.

Perhaps you believe you already know how to SEE, and perhaps you do. But there are deeper worlds of sight yet to be explored. The following demonstration can be easily used in a classroom; it is presented here in order to illustrate SEEING. Let me take you into a room and show you a picture. Let me show you the picture one hundred, maybe a thousand times. Then I will lead you out of that room and ask you a very basic question about what you saw. I predict you will not be able to answer that question. Ready?

The room is imaginary; on the wall blown up to huge dimensions are the four kings from an ordinary deck of playing cards. Imagine them in your mind's eye. You have seen them dozens, hundreds, thousands of times. I will not ask you for a tiny detail just yet; only for a basic observation. Picture the cards and select the one king that shows only one eye. DO NOT TURN THE PAGE UNTIL you have either answered this question or honestly admitted your inability to do so. . . . But try.

No doubt you have played cards, perhaps you have spent countless hours looking at the cards. Yet very likely you were not able to identify the one-eyed king. Those who can select the proper king are quite exceptional. Try this demonstration on your friends; very few of even the most fanatical card players will answer correctly.

How can this ignorance be explained? A case of poor memory? If the question is posed to people with exceptional memories, they fare no better than the statistical average of one in four.

You might want to use as an excuse the fact that you haven't played cards for a long time and therefore don't remember which king is which. Well, about one minute ago you looked at all four kings. Do not look

Visual Awareness

back at the cards. How else is the king of diamonds different from all the other kings? How is the weapon of the king of hearts different from the others? What is the king of hearts lacking that the other three possess? Take a look at the cards again; look for the answers and for other differences and similarities among the kings. As you do this, you are beginning (just barely) to SEE instead of to look.

As you examine the cards, you might ask why we call the card with this symbol ♣ a "club" and not a clover? Or why this symbol ♠ is called a "spade?" A little research into the history of playing cards will reveal the answers along with other information that will enable you to SEE more in the cards.

Quickly. Draw the shape of a baseball diamond in the box below.

Did you draw the diamond to look a little like the one on the playing cards? Many people do, especially those who have seen many baseball diamonds and should know better. A baseball diamond is a ninety-foot square and not diamond-shaped at all. Now we're back where we started. People who look at cards but see no details, people who look at squares and see diamonds. Why?

Perhaps this little experiment with playing cards can be considered a parable. The cards are like the world. We look at playing cards only long enough to label them and determine their value in the game. And so we never really see the cards . . . . We hear the phrase "baseball diamond" and so we think in terms of a diamond shape in spite of the evidence of our senses. How much of the world is like a deck of cards? This chapter is about the difficult art of SEEING, of becoming visually aware, eye-

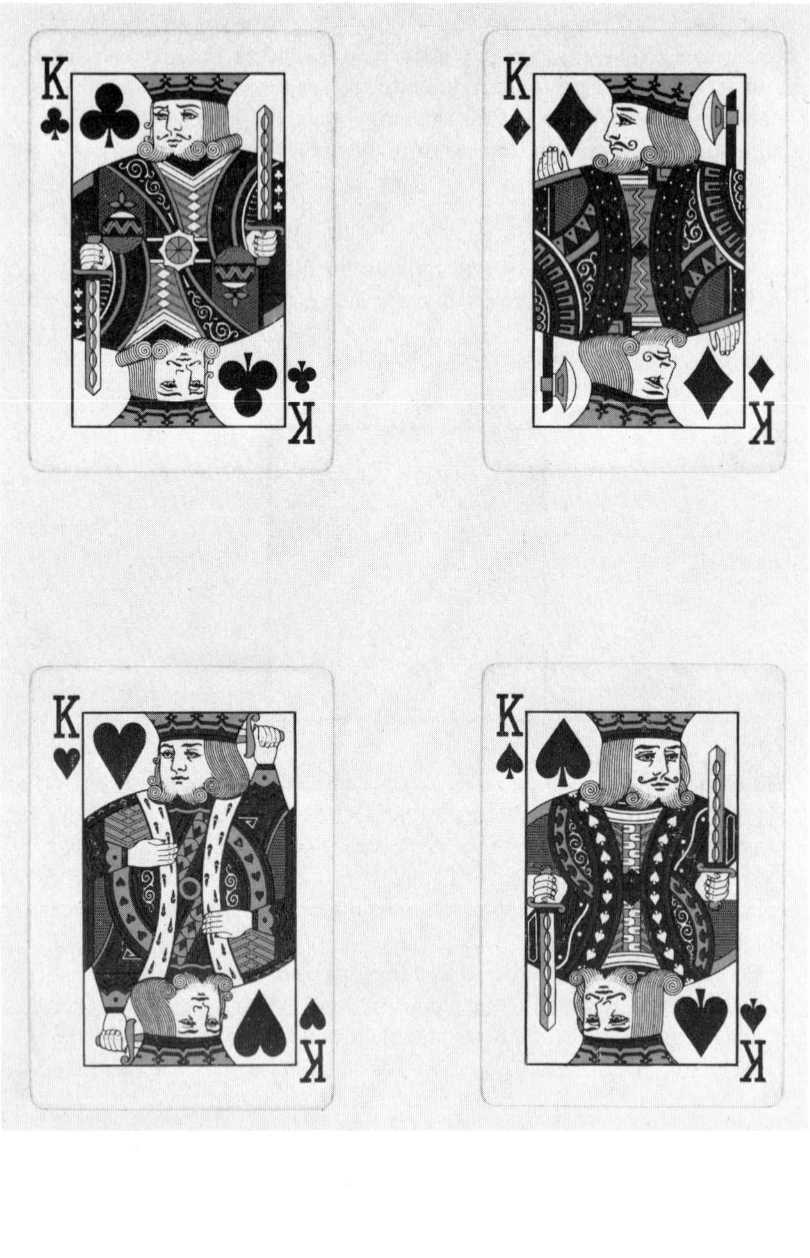
K
K
K
K

alive. Neither this book nor any teacher can manufacture visual awareness but this chapter can suggest that there is something out there in even the most commonplace objects yet to be SEEN.

The ideas which follow are not a well-constructed and well-designed building, they are more like a construction site. The ideas are not backed by funded research, but they have been used successfully in many schools and students have reported a bit less blindness after working with the activities. So don 'the hard hat of experimentation and join with your students in learning to SEE.

Since educators are not going to rush out and institute courses in visual awareness, the ideas here are designed to be incorporated in special electives, courses in creative writing, art, or even film study.

AN INTRODUCTION TO VISUAL AWARENESS

To introduce students to the blindness that afflicts every person to some degree, use the playing-card and baseball-diamond ideas described in the introduction to this chapter.

Or to begin on a more positive tone discuss with students moments of acute visual awareness. Many students can relate an experience of visual aliveness when a particular sight seemed to impress them beyond the boundaries of the ordinary.

To illustrate the gap between ordinary visual blindness and higher states of eye-awareness give the class a test concerning the room (or building) in which the course is held. Ask a series of questions such as what color the floor outside the door is; ask for a description of the wall at the students' back and descriptions of objects ordinarily in the room but hidden before class for this test. After such a test, on which students invariably miss many seemingly "obvious" questions, discuss reasons for the result.

Next conduct a visual survey of the room, having students note at least one example of each of the following:

> Something never before SEEN (eliminate people or artwork on wall as the subject of this survey).
> Something ordinary yet beautiful
> Something ugly
> Something to describe in detail.

The survey will take about ten minutes. After the survey period discuss some of the answers and have students describe some objects in the room in detail. A student might select a chair, for example. The descriptions should take the form of a series of statements beginning with the words "I see." The statements should not be of the "it is . . ." variety. Using the "I see" form emphasizes the fact that seeing is a creative activity.

If these visual-perception exercises take place in a writing course, some assignment can flow from the observations. Students could put their detailed descriptions in writing or be instructed to find and write about "There is something very beautiful in this school that no one ever notices. . ."

Seeing the Ordinary

This series of activities has not suggested viewing slides of the world's greatest masters or the best examples of current photography. The reason this has been avoided is that the point of this chapter is not to increase the appreciation or awareness of fine art, but to increase the enjoyment of the sense of sight. To help students understand this concept, present the following quotes for discussion.

> Do you know what impressed me most about America? How photogenic everything was. The blocks and blocks of used car lots and the endless freeways curling like gigantic snakes around the mountains. And the steel buildings shining through the clouds of pollution. The billboards — JESUS SAVES — DRINK PEPSI — all over. Americans are unaware of America! They eat hamburgers at a drive-in and stare out the car window but they don't see. Images are vital to me. They are strong and mysterious and they explain things to me about people
> —filmmaker Michelangelo Antonioni

> The visual sense in most men and women has been reduced to an economic minimum — the effort it takes to tell that the piece of paper is not a piece of bread, to tell when a parking space is not filled, to find the doors in a department store. A person who treats the world as a collection of objects that do not speak to him by their appearance will walk into a museum and see the paintings as mere objects. If he walks into a gallery he will see commodities and think of price tags. He will not be able to read the sensory statements. The esthetic sense has become atrophiec, and people expect a museum to offer a miracle cure. But if you do not already perceive the world with your senses you will not suddenly be seized with esthetic awareness when you walk through the doors of the Met.
> —Rudolph Arnheim, *Psychology Today*, interview, June 1972

Visual Awareness

> To see is to forget the name of the thing one sees.
>
> — poet Paul Valery

Looking and seeing both start with sense perception, but there the similarity ends. When I "look" at the world and label its phenomena, I make immediate choices, instant appraisals — I like or I dislike, I accept or reject, what I look at, according to its usefulness to the "Me" . . . THIS ME THAT I IMAGINE MYSELF TO BE, and that I try to impose on others.

The purpose of "looking" is to survive, to cope, to manipulate, to discern what is useful, agreeable, or threatening to the Me, what enhances or what diminishes the Me. This we are trained to do from our first day.

When, on the other hand, I SEE — suddenly I am all eyes, I forget this Me, am liberated from it and dive into the reality of what confronts me, become part of it, participate in it. I no longer label, no longer choose. ("Choosing is the sickness of the mind," says a sixth-century Chinese sage.)

—Frederick Franck, *The Zen of Seeing*

Learn to look long, to notice the breakup of shadows on a slat awning or the texture of a blacktop road. Try the child's-eye view of a dandelion or the close-up look of a tree. Forget measure, weight, price, bargain, and just LOOK at the supermarket or the stock exchange. SEE people, things with a first-time look.

—Jean Mary Morman, *Wonder Under Your Feet*

Shape Consciousness

Awareness of shapes as beautiful or meaningful in themselves is a visual skill that usually takes some training in art, drawing, or design to develop. But students can be given at least an introduction to shape consciousness by two simple exercises in abstraction.

For the first activity each student is randomly assigned a letter of the alphabet. Each must then find the shape of that letter existing either in nature or some found arrangement of objects and take a picture of the shape. The photo should be clearly a photo of the shape of the particular letter of the alphabet. For example, a picture of a tree in which many "V" shapes could be found is not acceptable. A picture of a two-trunked tree silhouetted against the sky would be acceptable. The ground rule to follow is that the *picture is the shape.* The assignment is *not* to take a picture in which a certain shape can be found. Encourage students to make the picture as unusual and creative as possible, especially for those students who draw the easier shapes (o, i, l, u, v).

Each person should take a number of pictures and then select the one which comes out best. Post the results and have a bulletin board of alphabet shapes. (An example of a photography student's approach to this assignment can be found in *Popular Photography* of May 1974, pp 66 ff.)

The purpose of the assignment is to encourage students to look at objects as abstraction of shape, to become more conscious of the shape of objects. For this reason the photos should be of "found" objects and not objects arranged to make a shape.

The second "shape awareness" exercise involves the recognition that typography sometimes expresses the meaning of the words used. Show a few book covers, magazine ads, or movie ads in which a typestyle is used to communicate or reinforce the meaning of the words. A few examples are given here.

We Bombed in New Haven is arranged in the shape of a bomb as an attention-getting device, a logo, and a reinforcement of the book's title.

On the cover of the book *Maverick Inventor* the CBS eye is shown tilted and "squashing" the words "maverick inventor." Without even reading the work one could correctly guess that the book is about an inventor who worked for CBS but had some disputes with the company. The typestyle chosen for the title is irregular as befits a "maverick inventor." The subtitle, "My Turbulent Years at CBS," is also reflected in the title and CBS eye above it.

Visual Awareness 137

—Harper & Row

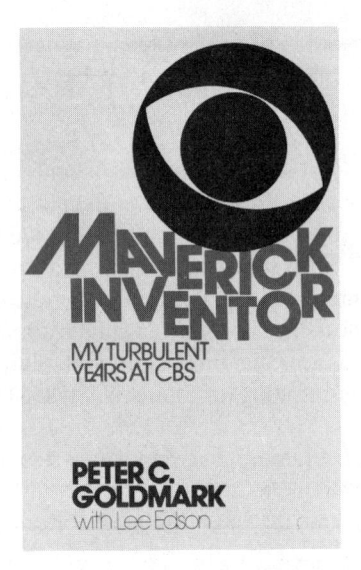

—Saturday Review Press

In the next book cover the typestyle chosen is a bit like that used in stencils where the letters often have lines that are disconnected. This particular typestyle was chosen to illustrate that "We, the Lonely People," are disconnected from each other. The four lines of print in the title come close to touching each other but never quite complete the connection. The curved lines that enclose the title are likewise separated by a gap and are incomplete. Thus the type is itself a statement of the theme of the book.

After showing a number of such examples to students have them find one book cover (or any other kind of graphic illustration) in which the letters are arranged, or the typestyle was chosen, to explain something about the book. This assignment encourages students to look beyond a casual glance at shapes usually taken for granted. The book cover can be found in any library and students should be aware that many or most books do not use type as creatively as the examples presented here. They may have to look at a dozen or more covers to find one that is suitable.

Have the students bring their examples to class and demonstrate how the typestyle and shape of other design elements on the book jacket contribute to or reinforce the book's theme.

Photoanalysis

The following suggestion of a class exercise to develop visual perception is inspired by Dr. Robert U. Akeret's Book, *Photoanalysis: How to Read the Hidden Psychological Meaning of Personal and Public Photographs.*

Akeret is a psychiatrist who has discovered family snapshots are as useful a tool in analysis as dreams. He uses the power of old photos to stir memories and bring back a deluge of feelings and buried associations. In *Photoanalysis* he offers some examples from his private practice and then moves on to interpret some two hundred photos of the famous: the large family of Rose and Joseph Kennedy in a revealing group photo, Richard Nixon's two faces, the three faces of Marilyn Monroe, the Roosevelts, and photo-readings of Churchill, Stalin, Truman, Picasso, Dali, and others.

Photoanalysis is useful in the classroom not as a tool for psychoanalysis but as a technique to urge students to really SEE photos. The first step in using "Photoanalysis" is to present to students a number of examples from Akeret's book along with his insights. The best way to do this is to enlarge the photos with an opaque projector. The book is in a hardcover edition from Peter H. Wyden, Inc., 750 Third Ave., New York, NY 10017. The book is also available as a Pocket Books paperback, but the photos are smaller and less sharp than in the hardcover edition.

At least a dozen of Akeret's photo interpretations make for good class presentations.

Have students bring to class three family snapshots. Two should be of a person or people that the rest of the class will not recognize; one snapshot should be of oneself taken at any time after infancy. The pictures should be snapshots, not professionally posed portraits. Each photo should be marked on the back, either with the owner's name or a code word, so they can be returned.

Redistribute the two photos of strangers among the class so each person has completely unfamiliar photos. Students can make this exchange on their own if desired. Each student retains the picture of him- or herself. Allow time for the students to look at the pictures for a long time and write an analysis of "What I see in this picture" for either one or both pictures. Discuss some of the insights as a class and have the person who knows the people in the picture confirm or deny some of the insights.

On the same day or perhaps later each student should perform an analysis of the self snapshot. This could be done by exchanging pictures again, but such a method often turns the class into a group of amateur psychologists analyzing each other rather than a group developing visual awareness.

Creating Visual Surprises

Familiarity breeds invisibility. Some object that is an often seen part of the environment tends to become invisible and unnoticed. The red-and-white Coca-Cola signs have become such an expected part of the contemporary environment that they are nearly invisible. People could walk down a street with twenty or more Coke signs and then be asked if they have seen a Coca-Cola sign and reply definitely, "No." For this reason Coca-Cola redesigned its signs so they were still familiar yet were different enough to be noticed.

To make the ordinary and unnoticed visually prominent it is sometimes only necessary to take it out of its ordinary context so that it becomes a surprise. The process of taking words out of context was dealt with in the previous chapter in regard to pop poetry. A similar kind of changing environments can be done with objects both to make them visible and to give them meaning.

To illustrate this concept to students show some of the paintings of René Magritte. Copies of his works are available in quality paperback books. One of the most noticeable and striking aspects of Surrealism is its unusual juxtaposition of objects that are rarely or never connected in reality. Surrealism expresses a philosophy, a way of viewing the universe to show "the poetry and mystery of subjects and their relationship to each other." Neither teacher nor student need understand the philosophy of Surrealism to see that creative paintings and photographs often use the element of surprise.

To students the pictures might simply be crazy, humorous, or weird. Show them as many examples of unusual visual juxtapositions as can be found from the works of Magritte, the photos in *Popular Photography, Modern Photography,* magazine ads and illustrations, record album covers or book covers. Have students try some of their own visual juxtapositions. Use photography, film, videotape, drawing, or magazine cutouts to create images that are exciting, unusual, weird, humorous, or just curious. Each image should illustrate visual surprise. There is no need for students to be able to explain the "meaning" of their particular juxtaposition.

In class swap the resulting images and have each student write a brief explanation of someone else's work. Tell students to assume each work is a serious piece of art and an attempt to communicate some truth.

The idea of visual surprise can go beyond the combining of images. When Andy Warhol painted pop pictures of Marilyn Monroe and Campbell Soup cans and when Claes Oldenburg sculpted huge plastic hamburgers, they created shock waves in the artistic community. But what they did is what artists throughout the ages have done to enhance vision — taking an image that cultured people considered beneath the dignity of art and placing it in a frame or a museum so that it could not be ignored by the appreciative eye.

To illustrate and experiment further with the idea of visual surprise and taking objects out of their normal context, design a class project to find some object in the school (or near the school) that goes unnoticed. The object should be one that is obvious, that has been there for a long time, but is relatively ignored. Devise some kind of creative juxtaposition, some kind of changed context, that will give the object a new visual life. Make it the talk of the school. The only rule for this project is that the object cannot be changed, only its context.

If the object is set up somewhere in the school, some class members could record student reactions to the "new" object. Collect reactions of students and discuss what the experiment reveals about SEEING.

A SERIES OF IDEAS FOR VISUAL EDUCATION BRIEFLY DESCRIBED

Kicking the Word Addiction Habit

The fact that you are now reading this book is probably a symptom of your addiction to words. Wordaholics are not a minority in Twentieth Century America, they are the norm. Schools teach word addiction and society uses this well-developed habit to sell and instruct, thus strengthening the dependence on words.

Ross Parmenter writes about his discovery of word addiction in *The Awakened Eye*:

> One beautiful spring day I took a train ride into the country. Although I was properly appreciative of the sky's soft blueness and the subtle bud colors that haloed the skeletons of the trees, my eyes, exasperatingly, kept snapping to the billboards. Almost invariably, in fact, when given a choice between an effect of nature and a sign, they would choose the sign. Since the city-dweller sees so little of the changing seasons this seemed a particularly trivial choice. Why, I asked, should I waste this precious opportunity of looking at spring trees in favor of reading about Mrs. So. and So's Snow-White Laundry?

The answer to the question lies in our training in the importance of words. We are so accustomed to the language of literacy that a word, any word, will attract the eye and claim its full attention. G. K. Chesterton remarked while walking in Times Square, "What a glorious garden of wonders this would be to anyone who was lucky enough to be unable to read." To the habitual word reader Times Square is merely a gaudy collection of signs; to the visually aware, non-addicted eye the sight would be a feast of colors, shapes and movement.

Conduct an experiment to help students realize their own tendency to word addiction. The experiment is to travel while looking out a window (perhaps on the way home from school) and yet to avoid reading any words. Students should, of course, be traveling through a landscape that has words, the more the better for the experiment. After the experiment discuss word addiction and the difficulty of non-reading. Also discuss how the habit of reading words can be a drawback to seeing.

Facades

The faces of buildings, like those of people, reveal personality. Assign students the job of looking at the facades of local buildings and houses — very old buildings and the very newest. Have them select two facades and either sketch or photograph them. One facade should illustrate what the student considers beauty and the other ugliness. Along with the photos or sketches have each student write a brief "personality sketch" of each building. The personality sketch should tell what the facade says to the world about the building.

Discuss only the Visible

Hold a classroom discussion with the single ground rule that only what is visible can be discussed. Discussion should not only be *about* visible objects but should be *limited* to those aspects of the object(s) that are visible now. A discussion about the imperfect glass in the classroom windows should not proceed to a discussion about glassmaking, for example.

Photo Imitation

Have each student find a photo to imitate. The photo could be from a magazine, an ad, or a photography magazine. The original should be a professional photo and not a family snapshot. The assignment is to try to take a photo that looks as much as possible like the original. If people appear in the original, it is permissible to replace them with other people. The imitation should not be done by taking a picture of the picture.

Students should be aware before this experiment that unless they are skilled in photography, their picture will look rather different from the original. This is not a lesson in photography, it is an experiment in vision. Allow several weeks at least for this assignment and encourage students to take more than one picture in an attempt to imitate.

When all the imitations are done, post them along with the picture being imitated and discuss how they are different. Each student should be able to give a detailed account (perhaps in writing) of how his picture and the original differ. Not *why* they differ, *how* they differ.

Postcards

If you live in or near a city large enough to sell a variety of picture postcards of city views, you can do a seeing experiment using the cards. Distribute to the class as many picture postcards as possible, eliminating only aerial views. Ideally, each student should have a different postcard, but this might not be practical.

Once the cards are distributed, each student is to find the exact spot from which the view on the card was photographed. This is to be done by taking the card to the place pictured and matching it with the view as it exists today. Once the spot is found, students should take notes on how the view has changed since the picture was taken. The changes, even the smallest, should be described in detail. If possible, have students take a photo of their own from the same spot and compare and contrast their photo with the postcard photo.

Record-Album and Book Covers

Earlier in this chapter we recommended having students carefully examine book covers to notice how typestyle is sometimes used to communicate. Another use for book and record-album covers is as items for visual analysis. Have each student select a record album or book cover to look at for a five- or ten-minute stretch. Then write or explain to the class why the cover contains the pictures or designs it does.

Color Awareness

Go to some local paint store and obtain sample chips of as many different colored paints as possible. If the paint samples are on cards, cut them into pieces so there is at least one for each student. Distribute the colors in class.

Each student is then assigned to seek as perfect a match as possible for his color. If the paint chips are labeled ("Champagne White," etc.), be sure students ignore the names given since they might tend to prejudice the response to the color. The match can be a fabric, printed matter, an object, a photo, anything except professional artists' colors.

The idea of the assignment is to have students be more aware of color differences at least while searching for the perfect paint-chip match. The matches should be shown and discussed in class. Again, the emphasis of the assignment should be on the *process* of viewing color rather than on the exactness of the final match. A most frequent result of this experiment is that students become aware, often for the first time, of the vast differences between shades of the basic color.

Photos

Assign students to shooting a roll of film, bringing the best picture to class.

A more structured assignment in creative looking is to present a list of "topics" for students to select from and photograph. A sample list might include:

Loneliness	Joy
Death	A shadow
Birth	Something invisible
Love	Wisdom
Fear	Something surprising
Ugliness	Something very important
Pure color	

It is important that in making this assignment the process of observation is stressed rather than the resulting photograph. Taking photos can actually be a visual deadener if the intention is only to produce an image that will elicit admiration from friends or teachers.

Capturing the Impossible

This idea was first presented by the Environmental Studies project sponsored by the American Geological Institute and supported by the National Science Foundation.

During a class period the students work alone so that each lists five things that are impossible to photograph. Then lists are exchanged and each student circles the two "impossibilities" that he or she believes are truly the most impossible. When this is completed, a simple assignment is given: Photograph either of the two impossible things you selected as the most impossible.

What Color Is Your City?

Hatami is a Persian-born photojournalist who has an unusual view of cities. He sees cities in terms of two-color themes. He sees the two colors as revealing much about a city's history and how it influences those who live there. London, he says, is red and black while New York is red and yellow. In each city he seeks out photos that illustrate the two-color themes. Examples of Hatami's work can be found in the January 1974 issue of *Popular Photography* (available in most libraries).

Have students select a two-color theme that best expresses the nature of one of the following:

> The city
> The school
> Their home
> Some other place

The two-color theme should not be selected until after the students have had time to look for one in the place they have chosen. The two colors should be those most often found *together*. Once they have selected a place and decided on which two colors best typify that place, then have students take color photos that express the color theme. If this is done in a creative-writing course, students could then write an explanation of the place in terms of the two colors.

Changing Vision

Have the class (and yourself) look at a painting (borrowed from a public library or a friendly lender) for about five minutes. If a painting is not available, use a slide as a last resort. Have students examine the picture very carefully during the five minutes.

When the time is up, place the picture out of sight and do something else (anything) for another five minutes. The "something else" should be totally unrelated to the painting.

Next have students attempt to see the painting in their minds in as full detail as possible. After students have done this for a minute or so, discuss the difficulty or ease of pictorial recall. Were there problems recalling certain objects, shapes, colors? Were there blank areas? (This experiment should not be presented as if it were an observation test.)

Now show the painting again and discuss with the class how it has changed from their imagined picture. Were parts left out or added? Discuss with the class the reason for the difference between the painting and the remembered image. Does vision almost always introduce or omit something from reality? Is vision a totally passive process like a camera or a human Xerox machine? Or is vision an active, creative process?

Ban the Cliché

In the chapter on creativity we saw how a written cliché conveys little information precisely because it is so expected. The same is true for pictures. Discuss with the class the idea of clichés with an emphasis on visual clichés. Have each student bring what he or she considers a "visual cliché" to class. Discuss visual clichés in films of television news. Be aware that no object, painting, photograph, or drawing is always a cliché. A pretty sunset, spooky house in a movie complete with thunder and lightning, a couple alone on a beach, or the Grand Canyon are not necessarily visual clichés. They are, however, if they are presented in a clichéd, often used manner that adds little insight to that which is already familiar.

To further help students recognize clichés and see what is creative in the visual arts, ban clichéd posters from the classroom and as much as possible from the school. Replace clichéd posters or paintings with the visually creative, the unusual, the striking and unfamiliar.

Books

The Awakened Eye by Ross Parmenter (Wesleyan University Press, Middletown, CT 06457; 1968) is a leisurely written exploration of the author's own rediscovery of the sense of visual awareness. For the patient, intelligent reader this is very likely the best single book on the subject of visual awareness. Although written in the form of a published autobiography, *The Awakened Eye* is a philosophy of aesthetics, a workbook for the eye, and a fascinating tool for developing one's own sense of visual aliveness. The playing-card idea used to introduce this chapter comes from Parmenter's book as do one or two of the activities suggested for the classroom. Highly recommended.

Experiences in Visual Thinking by Robert H. McKim (Brooks/Cole Publishing Co., 540 Abrego Street, Monterey, CA 93940; 1972, 170 pages) is designed for a college course in visual thinking. Developed and tested at Stanford University, the course helps teach perception, creative thinking, visualizing, sensing, seeing, and drawing. McKim uses an experiential approach throughout, resulting in a "workbook in visual thinking" with occasional readings.

Much of what McKim teaches is the same as that attempted by film and media teachers — to enable students to see. But McKim's approach is far more basic than merely teaching the language of the movie screen. He has readings and "experiences" about blocks to thinking, imagery, dreams, color, brainstorming, abstract-to-concrete thinking, fantasy, gestalt, grouping, imagination, muscle imagery, labeling, memory, pattern-seeking, perspective, projection, and much more. The book is highly recommended as a teacher resource for courses or units in creativity, film, imagination, writing, and art. Some high school teachers might even find it suitable as a student text.

The Hole Thing: A Manual of Pinhole Photography by Jim Schull (Morgan and Morgan, Inc., 145 Palisade Street, Dobbs Ferry, NY 10522; 36 pages) is a 36-page booklet that provides basic, understandable information for anybody who wants to learn photography without getting too confused by *f*-stops, TL's, SLR's, ASA's, and all that. A pinhole camera is simply a box with a pinhole letting light strike film. Certainly pinhole photography has limitations, but for learning about photography and visual language it is cheap, gives a clear and *basic* understanding of how photography works, and is completely do-it-yourself with fast results.

Using a 4" x 5" box for a camera, 400 negatives and positives can be developed from one 100-sheet box of 8" x 10" paper. The size of the box changes the focal length, thus allowing experimentation with wide-angle or telephoto-type pictures.

The Hole Thing gives complete, practical details on making a camera, taking pictures and developing them yourself. An excellent way for students of any age to learn about film, photography, or visual language.

Illusions: A Journey into Perception by Patricia Ann Rainey (Shoe String Press, 995 Sherman Avenue, Hamden, CT 06514; 1973) is a book about teaching perception. Designed for psychology or media literacy courses, Rainey's ideas and experiments could be useful for elementary through college level. Using optical illusions, color illusions, impossible objects, reversible figures, moiré patterns and spirals, Rainey analyzes their effects and suggests class experiments. Over 100 illustrations are included in the 109-page paperback.

Laughing Camera (Hill & Wang, 19 Union Square West, New York, NY 10003). Classroom walls deserve good photography, and humor wouldn't hurt either. *Laughing Camera* (volumes I and II) provides both inexpensively. Each book contains 72 pages of humorous photos printed on slick paper in a 7" x 9" hardcover format.

Not only could the photos be used to add life to bulletin boards and dull walls, they could also serve as part of a unit on the nature of humor or visual puns.

Painting With the Sun: A First Book of Photography (Dynamic Learning Corp., 60 Commercial Wharf, Boston, MA 02110; 1970, workbook and teacher's manual) is a small paperback that will intrigue a ten-year-old as well as parents who take an occasional snapshot.

The book could be read in ten minutes, but to work through its suggestions could take weeks. The workbook format gives basic pointers on taking pictures and suggests a series of photographic "problems" involving things, persons, places, and happenings. Following this are

Visual Awareness 149

more advanced yet simple ways to improve the viewpoint, lighting, and framing of photos.

A Primer of Visual Literacy by Donis A. Dondis (MIT Press, Cambridge, MA 02142; 1973, 194 pages, hardcover) is a scholarly introduction to visual design and communication. Although neither the typestyle nor the writing style in the book makes for the easiest possible reading, the approach of Dondis is thorough and clear for the reader willing to work a bit to learn. This book is not for high school students but could easily stand as required reading for teachers of any of the visual arts — from film to finger painting.

Dondis approaches visual language as a native tongue that students "know but cannot yet "read." Hundreds of illustrations are used to teach and clarify.

In the first fifty pages readers learn basic concepts, such as visual ambiguity. For example, which of the three illustrations below is the most ambiguous?

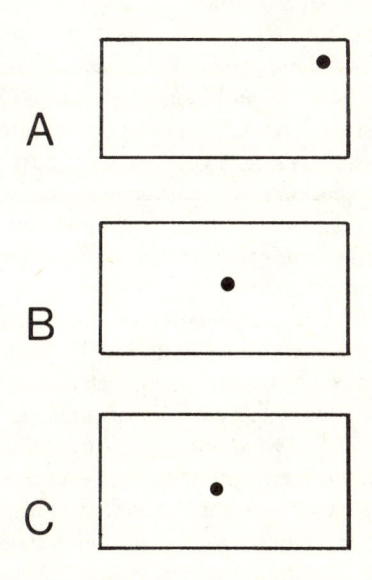

Perhaps you almost instinctively chose correctly (c), but can you explain visual ambiguity as well as you can verbal ambiguity; Or can you explain what a square means or the message of a circle?

The square, Dondis explains, communicates dullness, honesty, straightness, and workmanlike meaning; the circle suggests endlessness, warmth, and protection.

From such basic considerations, the primer moves through the basics of color, scale, abstraction, movement, contrast and harmony, and techniques for visual communication. Having established the basic vocabulary of visual language, the book applies the new concepts to visual styles of primitivism, expressionism, classicism, and others. With the vocabulary at hand each style's characteristics can be accurately summarized in fewer than a dozen words. The book concludes by exploring visual language in sculpture, painting, film, photography, and television.

A Primer of Visual Literacy is ideal for the teacher willing to expend time and effort to learn what might very well be the most important modern language of the near future.

Writing with Light: A Simple Workshop in Basic Photography by Paul Czaja (Chatham Press, 15 Wilmot Lane, Riverside, CT 06878; 1973, 96 pages, hardcover) is a stunning, young person's introduction to seeing and photography. In a simple yet sometimes poetic writing style Czaja deals with the beginnings of photography, the nature of light, making a simple camera out of a beach ball or box, developing film with hot salt water, taking photograms, and above all helping the reader to rediscover the joys of vision.

Photography, to Czaja, is a celebration of your seeing and the darkroom "a private place in which to see again." His chapter on light avoids the usual introductory-physics-book approach and instead invites readers to conduct a few simple experiments in observing light. He comments, "You will be a *good* photographer when you begin to take hold of the light that is there both with your eyes and with your feelings, and when you begin to care and wonder about it."

Even if you don't teach photography, this book should prove helpful in teaching any visual medium, especially film. The book is recommended for students and teachers alike, for in film and photography we are still beginners. And yet, so powerful has been the work from the pioneers of photography that already our generation prefers to see than to read. *Writing With Light* should help to refine that preference.

Wonder Under Your Feet: Making the World of Art Your Own by Jean Mary Morman (Harper & Row, 92 pages, paperback) guides readers through a collection of over 150 artworks always urging them to LOOK, wonder, and experiment with the ordinary. Each work of art is commented on with a few words that quickly turn into an encouragement to experiment with looking for the "breakup of form that is Op art in fire escapes, crystal reflections, shadow patterns, ripples on the water," or "Cut into a cabbage and find the busy excitement of a Baroque painting."

Wonder Under Your Feet is part sermon and part eye education urging students to "filter out enough of the media mess-age to see and hear for yourself." The book joins with G. K. Chesterton in reminding a media generation that "The world will never starve for wonders, but only for the want of wonder."

Other Resources

Fragments and *Looking and Listening*: *Fragments* is a set of 158 cards, each giving highly creative ideas useful in teaching perception or writing. The activities grew out of a course in "Visual Education" taught to high school students by artist Lowry Burgess. The cards are color-coded and grouped according to activities relating to Enduring Activities, Mapping and Representing, Sensory Awareness, Inner Landscapes, and Building and Making.

Looking and Listening is a set of 168 cards very similar to *Fragments*. This follow-up to the *Fragments* series deals with deepening the visual and aural perception and response. Burgess has used these exercises in classes from second grade through graduate level and in teacher training workshops. The cards are in three categories — Relationship of Images to Self, Problems and Perceptions Caused by Change, and More or Less Formal Concepts of Perception. Some of the *Fragments* exercises are duplicated in this set.

Samples of the kinds of ideas on the cards are presented here, admittedly out of context:

> *No. 60 – Looking Through One Eye and Then the Other:* Your two eyes see very differently (even if they are equally good). Look at an image first with one and then the other. Note down and share your observations. One eye may see lines better – the other may see color more brilliantly. Perhaps you might suggest that one eye is the sun and the other the moon.
>
> *No. 55 – Staring:* Stare at an image for a period of time without blinking. What begins to happen? What appears and disappears? What moves up and down from one side to the other? What does this activity develop inwardly? Stare at different works (paintings) for good periods of time. This will open new possibilities for looking and reveal some interesting visual rhythms.
>
> *No. 22 – Looking for Something Without Looking For It:* Can you tell your eye to look for a specific thing and let it? (Circular things or certain colors, even definite things.) E.g., you might say for the next two hours I am going to notice everything red. You should not look for red things, but allow your eye to notice them – to take you to them. Open yourself to them, feel yourself being dragged about by your eyes!
>
> *No. 131 – Describing What You Hear:* Can you describe what you hear? Describe it in minute details – making lists. Be specific. Keep describing what you've heard until you think you've described all you can and then do it some more. Share your descriptions. Everyone will be surprised at what they didn't hear.

The cards are available for about $10 per set from the Workshop for Learning Things, 5 Bridge Street, Watertown, MA 02172.

Environmental Communications is a Los Angeles distribution company with an unusual selection of color slides, films, books and videotapes concerned with such topics as architecture, art, and the environment. EC hopes to "turn people on to their own culture and legitimize those parts of real life that are often ignored but which nevertheless have great practical and theoretical relevance." Their materials are mostly slide series (average cost is $1 per slide) on parts of the environment like neon signs, murals, domes, West Coast contemporary architecture, and commercial architecture. The new catalog is 48 pages and among the most colorful and illustrative catalogs I've seen anywhere.

Everything EC has is expensive; even the catalog is $1.75; from Environmental Communications, 64 Windward Avenue, Venice, CA 90291.

Photography — How It Works is a simply written 20-page booklet from Kodak explaining how cameras work. The booklet is written for the very young but could prove useful in junior high. Single copies are free, multiple copies are 10c each. A free-loan ten-minute super-8 film based on the booklet is also available. Write Eastman Kodak Co., Dept. 841, 343 State Street, Rochester, NY 14650.

Allow the walls to speak. Many English and media classrooms have various colorful posters on the walls to add a little visual variety to the typically barren school environment. Often, though, these posters are visual clichés — nice, "pretty," competently photographed but still clichés. One would think that media teachers would consider it part of their "mission" to teach appreciation of the original and creative instead of the clichéd. With this in mind one source of wall hangings that are excellent teaching aids is a series of 11" x 14" photographic prints (not posters) of ten famous FSA photos. The portfolio includes Dorothea Lange's migrant mother, Walker Evans' sharecropper family, and Arthur Rothstein's farm couple holding produce. The complete portfolio of ten prints is $20 plus $1.50 postage and handling from K & L Custom Services, 222 East 44th Street, New York, NY 10017. Ask for the FSA portfolio.

Eye Openers is a program in writing/awareness developed by David Sohn and Don Blegen and distributed by Scholastic Books. The series consists of 93 color slides in a Kodak carousel, 48 black and white photos from the Kodak Teenage Photography Contest and a 40-page teaching guide.

The guide suggests a series of twenty assignments to help students write descriptions, figurative language, differing points of view, a mood paragraph, narration, dialogue, Haiku, character description, and finally a short story.

The slides are all fine as motivational devices although the photos (their use is left up to the teacher) are definitely more creative and visionary than the slides. The writing assignments progress from easy to more difficult. A typical assignment is to look at four slides and write a particular kind of paragraph.

Similar structures have often been used successfully in writing classes and the progression of assignments is sound. The unit is workable with almost any grade level. The first thirteen slides are used to "awaken the students' senses," as if watching the pictures in a darkened classroom is any way to develop sensual awareness. Teachers will have to rely on their own resources to add the third dimension to this otherwise fine unit.

The set is well packaged and sells for $74.50 from Scholastic Book Services, 904 Sylvan Avenue, Englewood Cliffs, NJ 07632.

Sight and Insight is a visual-education course consisting of filmstrips, taped commentaries, project books, and teaching notes designed to develop in students an awareness of their visual environment. The series is intended for high school and college level courses in art, visual education, design, photography, or even film study. The series was written by Kurt Rowland.

A preview copy of Package One (the entire set consists of four "packages," but each is available separately) shows the set to be of excellent quality with solid educational values. No frills in the production, fancy packaging, or excess baggage mar the set. Package One deals with "The Way We See," "Shape and Space," "Composition," and "Visual Communication" in four sound filmstrips and one project book.

Package One is the most valuable of the four packages for non-art-class students in high school and should help considerably in film study. The filmstrips are particularly strong when explaining how shape and space are positive parts of the visual environment (whether in a poster, film still, or painting). Package One is $60.

Packages Two through Four are a bit more technical and appear better suited for art students. A brochure or preview set is available from Van Nostrand Reinhold Company, 450 West 33rd Street, New York, NY 10001.

New Photographics '74 If the slides in the Scholastic Books *Eye Openers* are too dull or uncreative for you, try slide sets from *New Photographics '74*. The exhibit, sponsored by the Art Department of Washington State College, features the photographic work of 66 artists from across the country. The slides exemplify a fair cross-section of the directions photographic art is currently taking. Set 1 consists of 80 slides (at least one by each artist in the exhibit) and sells for $50 while all 240 slides are $120 from Roslyn Arts, Box 511, Roslyn, WN 98941.